"Our friend Gaye Clark has written a wi[...] term parental love. With engaging illustr[...] helps us care for our adult children more meaningful[...] helps us look to our Father God as we love our adult children. We—and they—are not alone in this journey."

Ray and Jani Ortlund, President and Executive Vice President, Renewal Ministries

"There are precious few resources to help guide parents in the launch phase of their parenting years. As a father of a child in college and three more soon to follow, I am thankful for the wisdom of this book. Being a mom or dad to an adult child is complicated and fraught with potential landmines. With experience, biblical wisdom, and grace, Gaye Clark helps families move into this new season of life. You will want this book in your library."

Daniel Darling, Director, The Land Center for Cultural Engagement; author, *A Way with Words*; *Agents of Grace;* and *The Dignity Revolution*

"We never stop being parents, but what does parenting look like when our children are grown? Gaye Clark's book, *Loving Your Adult Children,* is a gospel-saturated, grace-infused, and Christ-exalting look at parenting adult children. She points our gaze to the one who loves our children best. As a parent on the cusp of being an empty nester, I needed this book. You will too."

Christina Fox, counselor; speaker; author, *Like Our Father: How God Parents Us and Why That Matters for Our Parenting*

Loving Your Adult Children

Other Gospel Coalition Titles

Arlo and the Great Big Cover-Up, by Betsy Childs Howard

Confronting Christianity: 12 Hard Questions for the World's Largest Religion, by Rebecca McLaughlin

Does God Care about Gender Identity?, by Samuel D. Ferguson

Finding the Right Hills to Die On: The Case for Theological Triage, by Gavin Ortlund

Growing Together: Taking Mentoring beyond Small Talk and Prayer Requests, by Melissa B. Kruger

Keeping Your Children's Ministry on Mission: Practical Strategies for Discipling the Next Generation, by Jared Kennedy

Mission Affirmed: Recovering the Missionary Motivation of Paul, by Elliot Clark

The New City Catechism: 52 Questions and Answers for Our Hearts and Minds

Rediscover Church: Why the Body of Christ Is Essential, by Collin Hansen and Jonathan Leeman

Remember Death: The Surprising Path to Living Hope, by Matthew McCullough

You're Not Crazy: Gospel Sanity for Weary Churches, by Ray Ortlund and Sam Allberry

To explore all TGC titles, visit TGC.org/books.

Loving Your Adult Children

*The Heartache of Parenting and
the Hope of the Gospel*

Gaye B. Clark

:: CROSSWAY®

WHEATON, ILLINOIS

Loving Your Adult Children: The Heartache of Parenting and the Hope of the Gospel

© 2024 by Gaye B. Clark

Published by Crossway
        1300 Crescent Street
        Wheaton, Illinois 60187

Cover design: Amanda Hudson, Faceout Studios

First printing 2024

Printed in the United States of America

Trade paperback ISBN: 978-1-4335-8932-4
ePub ISBN: 978-1-4335-8934-8
PDF ISBN: 978-1-4335-8933-1

Library of Congress Cataloging-in-Publication Data

Names: Clark, Gaye B., 1963- author.
Title: Loving your adult children : the heartache of parenting and the hope of the gospel / Gaye B. Clark.
Description: Wheaton, Illinois : Crossway, 2024. | Includes bibliographical references and index.
Identifiers: LCCN 2023034432 (print) | LCCN 2023034433 (ebook) | ISBN 9781433589324 (trade paperback) | ISBN 9781433589331 (pdf) | ISBN 9781433589348 (epub)
Subjects: LCSH: Parent and adult child—Religious aspects—Christianity.
Classification: LCC BV4529 .C5215 2024 (print) | LCC BV4529 (ebook) | DDC 248.8/45—dc23/eng/20231204
LC record available at https://lccn.loc.gov/2023034432
LC ebook record available at https://lccn.loc.gov/2023034433

Crossway is a publishing ministry of Good News Publishers.

BP   33   32   31   30   29   28   27   26   25   24
15   14   13   12   11   10   9   8   7   6   5   4   3   2   1

This book is dedicated to Carolyn Alcorn Clark.
Thank you for teaching me how to love my adult children.

Contents

Introduction

Children and Their Parents

Long nights battling colic. Finagling a sick child to take his medicine—and not throw it up. Crawling out of the store with a screaming toddler because he did not get the toy he demanded. Changing the messy diaper of an eighteen-month-old acrobat who leaves you covered in poop.

Experiencing events like these while the radio played "You're Gonna Miss This" was laughable, until we realized Trace Adkins told us the truth. We blinked, and it happened. They grew into adults.

What is an adult child? Isn't the term itself a bit of an oxymoron? A simplistic answer might be an eighteen-year-old, or in some states, a twenty-one-year-old. For the purposes of this book, I will be discussing adult children as biological or adopted children of parents who are twenty-one years old and up, living outside the home, and financially independent from their folks. However, I use adolescents and adult children who still live in the home as illustrations as well. I acknowledge those who live under a parent's roof are under a separate set of obligations from those who do not. Yet, the twenty-four-year-old may have more in common with an eighteen-year-old than he might like to admit.

Becoming Adults

Becoming an independent adult is far more nuanced than some may think. A child may legally become an adult at eighteen, however, a certain part of the brain—the prefrontal cortex—isn't fully developed until he's closer to twenty-five. The prefrontal cortex is responsible for reasoning, planning, attention, and focus. It helps us control our emotions and facilitates our sense of judgment.[1] We also use it to understand and predict the consequences of our actions. When your teenage daughter is pulled over for going seventy miles an hour in a forty-five zone and says, "I don't know how this happened," she isn't completely off her rocker.

But when you give her consequences (and you should), you are helping her prefrontal cortex develop. Knowing this detail about her brain development might also keep you from rolling your eyes, at least a little.

While the twenty-four-year-old who is living on his own and the eighteen-year-old living at home are in different circumstances, they can both benefit from parental involvement. Wisdom on the parent's side is knowing how much involvement to have and when, especially where the twenty-four-year-old is concerned.

In this book we'll see how troubles that remain unresolved in childhood and adolescence can come calling as our children mature into adults. With grown or nearly grown adult children, it

---

1   Mariam Arain, Maliha Haque, Lina Johal, Puja Mathur, Wynand Nel, Afsha Rais, Ranbir Sandhu, and Sushil Sharma, "Maturation of the Adolescent Brain," *Neuropsychiatric Disease and Treatment* 9 (2013): 449–61.

can be easy to despair and think it is too late to improve or repair our relationship with our kids, too late to communicate our love for them in a way they can hear and receive. But is anything too difficult for God?

This is a book for parents of adult children, and yet it may also benefit parents of younger children. It is not a book on how to parent per se. Rather, it is an invitation to renew your love for Christ and shows how that love can inform your parenting. Our vertical relationship with God is the single most valuable tool for enhancing our horizontal relationship with our children.

The Goal for Christian Parents

We are all broken vessels—sinners. We have all failed to live up to God's perfect standards and need his mercy just as much today as the moment we came to Christ. His grace alone saved us, and we need to keep that in mind as we parent our children: he alone can save them, too.

When it comes to righteousness before God, we are not superior to anyone, including our kids. In the battle for their souls, we should be fighting not against our children but beside them. We fight a common enemy: sin and unbelief.

Christians don't primarily raise their children to become fully functioning adults, although that is part of their task. Instead, their primary aim is to teach their children to place their hope in God alone through the finished work of Jesus Christ. It would be tragic to bring up a child who was able to obtain an excellent job, marry, and raise a beautiful family—become someone who was considered an upstanding member of his community—but does not have a life-giving relationship with Jesus Christ, "for what does it profit a man to gain the whole world and forfeit his soul?" (Mark 8:36).

The Christian parent of an unsaved adult child has the same mission. He continues to pray and point his adult child to Christ as he is given opportunity. Since none of us know God's exact plan for our children's lives, we can pray, press on, and when weary, lean on our brothers and sisters in Christ. We should not feel like a failure, for none of us know God's timing in salvation, even when it comes to our kids. His plans and purposes extend far beyond our desires.

Overall, God gives sinful moms and dads the difficult task of bearing witness to the salvation that can be found in Christ, trusting him completely with the outcome. This gives parents reason to cry out to God for the grace needed to refine their own hearts first before they seek to reprove their children. Part of evangelizing their kids is modeling what repentance looks like in their own walk with Christ. "First tak[ing] the log out of [their] own eye" (Luke 6:42) would be a great place to start.

In short, *Loving Our Adult Children* uses key components of the gospel (faith, repentance, forgiveness, and grace) as well as the fruit of the Spirit to enhance your relationship with Christ and, as a result, strengthen the bond with your adult child. It is my hope this book will point both you and your adult child to an everlasting love, an everlasting hope: Jesus Christ.

1

Faith

WHERE DID THE TIME GO? This quintessential question grips us and messes with our emotions. One car brand captured this feeling perfectly in a commercial that featured a little blond-haired boy who packs up his belongings and puts them into the back of the family car.[1] His faithful puppy tags behind. The boy returns to his room for another load. Something feels strange here. His dad, looking out into the hall from a bedroom, raises an eyebrow when he notices an oversized box making its way down the stairs. Then he sees his son juggling the massive package and struggling to keep it upright.

"Buddy, you need some help?"

"No. I'm good."

A family photo catches the boy's eye. He stops, adds it to the box, and then heads for the car. As I watch, the knot in my gut

---

[1] Subaru of Englewood, "2017 Subaru Impreza, Subaru Commercial, Moving Out," YouTube Video, https://www.youtube.com/. All quotations in this section are from this source.

tightens. In the garage, Mom clutches a stuffed animal she found in an old chest full of toys. She rummages through the other treasures.

"Hey, do you want these?"

"Why don't you keep those, Mom?"

He drags a blanket to the car, but his dog pulls it back toward the house. The boy tugs the blanket in return. "Come on, Moe. I have to go."

Where is this little fella going, and why don't his parents stop him? His folks join him at the car; an open trunk obscures the view. When Dad shuts the trunk, he and his wife have aged fifteen years. They turn to hug their son, who has transformed into a young adult. The young man then stoops to pet his beloved old dog. "See ya later, Moe."

The narrator, voice tender with emotion, says, "We always trusted our Subaru would be there for him someday. We just didn't think someday would come so fast."

The vehicle pulls away from the drive, his parents hold each other as they watch the car drive out of sight, and the word "love" closes out the one-minute spot. Cue the tissues because we're all a mess just watching.

Hidden Idols

No pain grabs us quite like parental pain. It seizes our hearts as we raise our children, but more so as they embark on the grand adventure called adulthood. We roll back the video of our kids' childhood, smile at the happy times, and, if we're honest, wince at things we regret. Some of us even weep. Is it too late?

Through tears, this is what I've heard parents say: "He's all I've got," "If I lost my daughter, you'd have to just put me in a mental institution," "He's my heart and soul," and "They are everything to me."

When you have a healthy relationship with your adult children, all can seem right with the world. Research has borne this out— "young adults and their parents perceiving their relationship as good has been associated with low psychological distress and high life satisfaction."[2] But parents and adult children don't always agree on the state of their relationship.

Parents may believe their relationship is healthier than their adult kids think it is,[3] and this mismatch can blindside them when an adult child cuts off communication. One study found that "1 in 4 U.S. adults have become estranged from their families."[4] A *Journal of Marriage and Family* article reported that 11 percent of mothers ages sixty-five to seventy-five with two or more grown children were estranged from at least one of them.[5] Clinical psychologist Dr. Joshua Coleman, who surveyed 1600 estranged parents, explained in an interview,

> Ironically . . . estrangement happens because the adult child is in some ways too loved, too taken care of. And one of

2 Debra Umberson, "Relationships between Adult Children and Their Parents: Psychological Consequences for Both Generations," *Journal of Marriage and Family* 54, no. 3 (1992): 664–74.

3 Jane B. Lancaster, Jeanne Altmann, Alice S. Rossi, and Lonnie R. Sherrod, eds., *Parenting Across the Life Span: Biosocial Dimensions*, 1st ed. (London, UK: Routledge, 1987), chap. 15.

4 Tamara Markard, "When the Ties that Bind Are Cut: The Silent Epidemic of Parental Estrangement," *Greeley Tribune*, June 11, 2022, https://www.greeleytribune.com/.

5 Megan Gilligan, J. Jill Suitor, and Karl Pillemer, "Estrangement Between Mothers and Adult Children: The Role of Norms and Values," *Journal of Marriage and Family* 77 (May 2015): 908–20.

the consequences of a much more intensive, anxious, guilt-ridden, worried, involved parenting that has been going on in the past three or four decades is that sometimes adult children get too much of the parent, and they don't know any other way to feel separate from the parent than to estrange themselves.[6]

Getting too much of a parent—resulting from what is referred to as "helicopter parenting" and identified by a lack of boundaries—is the most common (but certainly not the only) reason adult children distance themselves from their parents. Yet how could caring—or caring too much—for the children God gave us be wrong? Christian counselor Christina Fox writes, "There is a fine line between doing all the necessary things to care for and raise our children and making all that we do be about them."[7] Our outward behavior has an inward motivation. And it all goes back to what or who we treasure.

Worship God Alone

Who are we supposed to treasure? More specifically, who are we to treasure the most? The psalmist writes, "Whom have I in heaven but you? And there is nothing [and no one] on earth that I desire besides you" (Ps. 73:25). Could desires for our children actually be a turning away from this kind of worship, an idolatry?

6   Rebecca Rashid and Olga Khazan, "Parents Are Not All Good and Bad," *Atlantic*, June 6, 2022, https://www.theatlantic.com/.

7   Christina Fox, *Idols of a Mother's Heart* (Fearn, Scotland: Christian Focus, 2018), 105.

Tim Keller defines idolatry as

> anything more important to you than God, anything that
> absorbs your heart and imagination more than God, anything
> that you seek to give you what only God can give. A counterfeit
> god is anything so central and essential to your life that, should
> you lose it, your life would hardly be worth living. An idol has
> such a controlling position in your heart that you can spend
> most of your passion and energy, your emotional and financial
> resources on it without a second thought.[8]

Fox offers a similar definition of idols as turning to another source
for "things only God can provide."[9]

Overall, parents need both the truth of God's word and his love
to care for their kids without making them an idol. If we point
our kids to Christ as we raise them, we will reinforce our primary
devotion to God as we offer our children life-giving love and care.
Some parents think they can teach their kids the gospel by simply
taking them to church. But it isn't just the church who will give
an account before God concerning the care of children—it is
primarily mom and dad.

So how are parents doing in this area? What kinds of regular
conversations are they having about Jesus with their kids? Do
children know how their parents came to Christ? Do children
know how God is working in their parents' lives now? Are parents
willing to share some of the mistakes they've made and how God's

---

8   Timothy Keller, *Counterfeit Gods: The Empty Promises of Money, Sex and Power, and the Only Hope That Matters* (New York: Dutton, 2009), xix–xx.
9   Fox, *Idols of a Mother's Heart*, 56.

grace transformed them? Far from making them appear weak in their kid's eyes, conversations like these can strengthen the bond between parent and child. These conversations empower parents' faith in God because they remind parents that they are flawed vessels, dependent on the Lord to accomplish anything redemptive.

Model Empathy

A friend, Russel, expressed frustration because his son made careless errors in math that could have easily been avoided if he had only double-checked his work. His son, who tended to rush through many things, didn't seem convinced that looking over his work would make a significant difference in his grade, let alone a difference in life outside of math class.

Around that time, Russ's family had to postpone a long-anticipated family vacation. The reason? When balancing his checkbook, Russel had made a math error several weeks earlier. He added an entry that should have been subtracted. When he finally caught the error the following month, several hundred dollars he thought he had saved for the vacation just weren't there.

He decided to use his own mistake to help his son. With tears in his eyes, he said, "It's my fault we must postpone our vacation."[10] He explained his error and how he'd forgotten to double-check his work. "This is just one area where math will matter outside of class, son." Without any lectures or ultimatums, his son's efforts in math improved. Sometimes we can more effectively point out our child's shortcomings by using empathy instead

10 All quotations in this chapter and following that do not have citations are from the author's personal experience.

of condemnation. Loving God first includes bringing children "up in the discipline and instruction of the Lord" (Eph. 6:4), but discipline isn't always negative. It can also mean affirming our children when they do right.

Eyes to See the Good

When a mom came by to speak with me about her adult son, she said, "He won't talk with me." I happened to know both her and her son well. Mom was a demanding parent who had unrealistic expectations of her children. I asked her, "When was the last time you affirmed your son about anything he said or did? Even the smallest thing would do." She told me she didn't know of anything positive to praise. Ouch. No wonder her son refused to speak.

When we are angry with our kids or feel disappointed by them, it can be hard to see the positive. We need to pray for God to give us eyes to see past our frustration and annoyance. Sometimes amazing gifts hide amid the mess.

Historians call Benjamin West one of the great masters among American artists. His paintings line the halls of museums in America and Great Britain. In 1745, when he was seven years old, his mother asked him to look after his baby sister, Sally. When his sister fell asleep, he gathered his ink, paintbrush, and paper and began to work. His tools were homemade and weren't neatly contained in airtight containers or ziplock bags. Ink spilled everywhere.

His mother's return startled him. She surveyed the mess in front of her, but she was able to see beyond the obvious chaos of a child's unsupervised creativity. She picked up Benjamin's "masterpiece" and said, "Why, it's Sally!" and kissed him.[11] Benjamin West later remarked, "My mother's kiss made me a painter."[12] Benjamin West's mother could have scolded her son and unwittingly frustrated his budding talent. But she didn't. Instead, she had eyes to see the good.

Don't Exasperate Your Children

In that same verse in Ephesians where Paul speaks of discipline and instruction he writes, "Fathers, do not exasperate your children" (6:4 CSB). Most dictionaries define "exasperate" as having strong feelings of irritation or annoyance. It builds up slowly over time with this significant wrinkle of misery: when we are exasperated, we feel as though there isn't anything we can do to alleviate the circumstance.

Consider a teenager who said the loaded phrase, "But I can explain!" to which his mom raised her hand and said, "I don't want to hear it. I've listened to your nonsense too many times before." Mom had heard his share of excuses. But parents aren't mind readers. She *didn't* know what her son was going to say that day. He might have been about to give another lame excuse, or this might have been a different circumstance entirely. Unless mom was clued in by a dependable eyewitness, she ought to have at least heard him out. But she opted to cut him off instead.

And the son? He concluded that his mom not only refused to listen but also didn't care. That's exasperation. Over time, it can boil over into fury.

---

11 Richard W. Leeman, ed., *African American Orators: A Bio-Critical Sourcebook* (Westport, CT: Greenwood, 1996), 176.
12 Leeman, *African American Orators*, 176.

Parents exasperate their kids when they focus only on rules (or personal preferences) above their relationship with God or overdiscipline their kids in the name of holding them accountable. One way these can happen is when parents misunderstand their child's developmental capabilities associated with his current age and place unreasonable expectations on him because they believe he is "wise beyond his years." It's possible for any child to display extraordinary wisdom in a given circumstance, but all of us need time to grow up properly in Christ.

Children can also become exasperated if their parents underdiscipline them. These parents could be blind to their child's behaviors or simply have no idea how to address a particular behavior. As a result, their children grow up having no idea where the boundaries lay. This isn't an exhaustive list, but one can begin to consider ways parents might exasperate their children.

Of course, Paul's words in Ephesians do not mean that a parent must never make his children mad. Children (and adults, for that matter) don't especially like being told no, even if it is for their own good. Sometimes children will be angry because their parents are being godly parents. Further, when dealing with adult children with an exceptionally long history of self-absorbed behavior, blame-shifting answers for their actions, there may come a time when it would be wise to no longer be willing to hear them out until you see evidence of repentance. Yet, this action shouldn't be taken in the heat of frustration but only after serious prayer and seeking appropriate counsel.

Don't Lose Heart

Navigating a balance between allowing our children the freedom to grow and flourish while at the same time disciplining them when necessary is not for the fainthearted. Parents of an adult child may feel they have done all these things to the best of their ability but their son still isn't walking with the Lord. They are devastated when they hear him speak as confidently of his unbelief as they do about their Savior. Where is their hope now?

In Habakkuk 2, God assures the prophet, "the vision awaits its appointed time. . . . If it seems slow, wait for it; it will surely come; it will not delay" (Hab. 2:3). Sometimes parents will have to white-knuckle their fingers around the promises of God's word and not let go. They must keep trusting a loving and merciful God to order the ways of their child. In so doing, they remind themselves that they worship the Lord, not their children.

Later in this book, you will read a mother's story who kept bringing her son before the Lord and almost drove her pastor crazy—yet never wearied her God. The fruit of her prayers benefited not only her son but thousands of Christians for centuries afterward.

Be about discovering the mercies of God. Scripture says his mercies are "new every morning" (Lam. 3:23). Every morning pursue them—to your last breath. Lost children can still come to Christ after the death of a parent. We must keep our eyes fixed first and foremost on God, not our adult child.

Hidden in Plain Sight

We know better than to place our children in a position where only God should be, but has that exchange perhaps taken place without our knowledge? Like the hidden fees on my cable bill, idols have a way of creeping into our lives and costing us more than we know. Where our children are concerned, idols can be years in the making. When we think of idols, we might think of evil gods such as Molech, a Canaanite deity associated with child sacrifice in the Old Testament (Lev. 20). When we consider idolatry, the hideous transformation of the hobbit Sméagol to Gollum in the *Lord of the Rings* trilogy comes to mind. But Satan can be more subtle with false gods and worship.

If we have idolized our children, one occasion God may use to reveal our idolatry to us is when our children sin. When we're angry because an adult child is dating someone outside our beloved church denomination, are we just as angry about what is going on inside our hearts? Is our concern unadulterated zeal for the Lord, or are we angry that our kid's behavior smashed to pieces our image of a perfect family?

If our kids fail us, it can be difficult not to take their failure personally. How about if they disrespect us? That *is* personal. And what if they opt for something we do not approve of but isn't sin? Paul Tripp writes about one aspect of treating our children as idols when he says,

> We begin to need [our children] to be what they should be so that we can feel a sense of achievement and success. We begin to look at our children as our trophies rather than God's creatures. We secretly want to display them on the mantels of our lives as visible testimonies of a job well done. When they fail to live up to our expectations, we find ourselves not grieving for them, but angry at them, fighting against them, and, in

fact, grieving for ourselves and our loss. We're angry because they've taken something valuable away from us, something we've come to treasure, something that has come to rule our hearts: a reputation for success.[13]

Loving God for Himself

Idolatry sometimes manifests as misplaced love. One of my favorite people in the Scriptures is Leah, the ugly girl who no one wanted. Leah's father, Laban, pawned her off to Jacob in marriage with a bait-and-switch scheme as if she were a cheap consolation prize on *Let's Make a Deal*. I can't imagine the mixed emotions Leah must have felt on her wedding day, her face heavily veiled, seeing a beaming groom but knowing he was thinking of her sister.

Leah's sham wedding and honeymoon lasted only a week before Laban allowed Jacob to marry Rachel as well. Leah would live the rest of her married life as an unwanted spouse. But when the Lord saw Leah was unloved, he opened her womb and closed Rachel's. So Leah tried to heal the searing wound in her heart with children. She named her firstborn Reuben, meaning "to see." She hoped God would open her husband's eyes to her worth through this new baby, saying, "Now my husband will love me" (Gen. 29:32).

Only he didn't. My heart breaks every time I read those words. I've known moms who had children with this misguided hope that the babe would heal the marriage. But the parents who despair of their marriages and now focus solely on a grown child harm both themselves and their children. Often these children grow up to become adults who complain that their parents have never

---

13 Paul Tripp, "The Idol of Success," *Paul Tripp Ministries* (blog), May 3, 2013, https://www.paultripp.com/.

learned boundaries and pry into areas of their lives where they were not invited.

Leah had another son named Simeon, which means "hear." Would Jacob listen? No. Then a third came, Levi, meaning "attach." Finally, Leah hoped, her husband would connect to her in a deeper way. But he did not.

Yet, Leah was no quitter. She redoubled her efforts with each pregnancy. She may have been struggling but she hadn't quit talking to God and seeking to understand where he was in her circumstances. At Reuben's birth, she rejoiced "because the LORD has looked upon my affliction" (29:32). With Simeon's birth, she had claimed, "the LORD has heard that I am hated" (29:33). She persisted.

Remember Tim Keller's definition of idolatry: "Anything that you seek to give you what only God can give."[14] Leah was hoping to get her husband's love and attention through her children. But even if her plans had proven successful, Jacob was woefully inadequate to give her what her heart truly longed for. No spouse or child can fulfill our deepest needs. Only God can do that.

A fourth son Leah named Judah, which means "praise." This time, she did not mention her husband. No; she said, "This time I will praise the LORD" (29:35). At last, the goal wasn't her husband's love. She learned what it meant to rest in the love of God alone and found him satisfying. God had always seen her as beautiful. He had always heard her, and he was the God who would never leave nor forsake her. He alone was worthy of her praise.

14 Keller, *Counterfeit Gods*, xix.

What profound comfort Leah must have found in knowing this. Only God can heal the ache in our hearts when disappointments tempt us to turn to our children for things they can't give us.

Our Children Belong to the Lord

Hannah had similar circumstances to Leah's. Her husband's other wife, Peninnah, ridiculed her, not for her lack of beauty but because Hannah was barren. First Samuel tells us that Hannah's "rival [Peninnah] used to provoke her grievously to irritate her, because the Lord had closed her womb. So it went on year by year" (1 Sam. 1:6–7).

Year by year. Many parents relate to trials that never stop. Hannah endured Peninnah's cruelty for years, taking her grief to the Lord in prayer. She asked him for a son. In return, she promised to "give him to the Lord all the days of his life" (1:11).

Did we read the passage correctly? She asked God for a son so she could give him back to God. Who would make that promise after years of infertility?

Hannah wanted a child—but not to shut Peninnah's mouth, remove the cultural shame, or satisfy a legitimate maternal desire. She wanted to bear a child who would live for the glory of God. Could Hannah trust God with her child? Yes. But she didn't get there overnight. God worked this surrender in Hannah through the years of suffering she endured. His plans were far greater than she could imagine. Thus, for Hannah, it was no longer about her desire alone but about God's plan working through her desires.

Scripture says that "in due time, Hannah conceived and bore a son, and she called his name Samuel, for she said, 'I have asked for him from the LORD'" (1:20). Then, when Hannah weaned Samuel (around age three), she kept her promise and brought him to Eli the priest. She went up to the temple with her son and all his belongings and returned with empty arms.

She could have gone home in tears. Instead, in the next chapter of 1 Samuel we see a woman bursting forth with praise to God. Hannah made a holy transaction: she traded her heartaches and a hope centered on her world for God's plan, purposes, and kingdom. She meditated on God's attributes, character, and promises. She asked that her desires become molded to his plan.

As I read of Hannah bringing Samuel to Eli, my mind floods back to my son's wedding day. Weddings can be hard for the mother of the groom. My son, Nathan, made a vow to his beloved bride to love her above all others—which included me. That is how it should be, but parents can struggle to let go. As I watched my son and his bride pledge their love and fidelity to God and to each other, I prayed they would live to glorify God and I would take hold of the faithfulness of God. During this time of transition for us, I could trust God with these two precious lives. They'd always belonged to the Lord.

Do we see our adult children as belonging to us or the Lord? Often, we can find the answer as we retrace our steps and consider the state of our heart through their earlier years. Idolatry with our children can be seen when we make them the center of our world or expect them to give us something that only God can give. We can also see idolatry revealed in our hearts if we struggle to relinquish control of our children when it is time for them to leave us.

Every fall, parents load their minivans with their beloved college students along with their belongings and head to campuses all over the country. They will come back with an empty vehicle after what is sure to be a longer drive home than it was there. For many, it's a bittersweet moment filled with tears and happy memories. But for some, it can be a very trying time. They had centered their entire world around their child, and now that child is gone. An empty nest, for these parents, means an empty heart. They just feel lost. Again, Keller's words on idolatry warn us: "should you lose it [an idol], your life would hardly be worth living."[15] If this is your story, ask God to grant you repentance and open your heart to loving him alone as your God. There could be no better comfort for this kind of pain.

Restoring True Worship

Overall, part of why we are so prone to idolatry is that we think so little of Christ. When we do think of him, it might be a false Jesus we contemplate. In, Colossians, Paul speaks of the preeminence of Christ, unfurling the beauty of the incarnation and the image of God. This passage is worthy of your memorization because it captures Christ's essence as the visible representation of the invisible God. It says that Jesus

> is the image of the invisible God, the firstborn of all creation. For by him all things were created, in heaven and on earth, visible and invisible, whether thrones or dominions or rulers or authorities—all things were created through him and for him. And he is before all things, and in him all things hold

---

15 Keller, *Counterfeit Gods*, xx.

together. And he is the head of the body, the church. He is the beginning, the firstborn from the dead, that in everything he might be preeminent. (Col. 1:15–18)

"The firstborn of all creation" does not mean that Jesus is a created being. No; Jesus is the *heir* of all creation. He owns it all. And when you ponder his ownership, consider this: Jesus owned the wood and nails that created the cross that crucified him. He owned the real estate we know as Calvary. He owned the robe the soldiers placed on him to mock him. He owned the thirty pieces of silver the religious leaders gave to Judas to betray him.

In the next verses of Colossians, Paul gives further evidence that he does not mean Jesus is a created being when he writes that "by him all things were created" (1:16). If Jesus created all things, he could not have been created. Consider, too, the scope of creation: things "in heaven and on earth, visible and invisible, whether thrones or dominions or rulers or authorities" (1:16). Jesus created every square inch of anywhere we can imagine.

Further, "he is before all things, and in him all things hold together" (1:17). I forget this when I leave the house with the weight of the world on my shoulders, thinking I am the one who must hold it together. Most mornings, I can't even find my car keys.

What are you trying to hold together? What are you trying to control in the name of loving your adult son or daughter? And how is that working for you? When we ponder these verses on who Christ is—all that he owns, his power, glory, and honor—we would be fools not to place our full confidence in him. We care for our horizontal relationships best when we nourish our vertical relationship with God first. When we rest in Christ alone, we can cry out to God instead of railing against our adult children about their sins or pacing the floor over how to fix what we cannot control. Christ alone can be the Savior.

Have you considered how magnificent your Savior is? How he longs to take from you the reins of control you cling to? Do you see what a superior God he is compared to the gifts he given you? Place your faith in him alone. You can trust him.

Discussion Questions

1. Do you feel like your children grew up fast? What experiences have made you most nostalgic for their younger years?

2. In what ways can our children become idols?

3. How can we love and care for our adult children without making them idols?

4. How can our emotions help us identify idols in our hearts?

5. Is letting go of your children difficult for you? How can meditating on the greatness of Christ help you let go?

6. What "impossible circumstance" can you relinquish control of in order to acknowledge Christ as the one true God who owns all things?

7. Read Psalm 121. What question does the psalmist ask and what is the answer? List the truths that the psalmist proclaims about God. Why is knowing God essential to worshipping him?

8. How does understanding God's nature and work reorient your focus as a parent?

2

Repentance

"I HATE YOU." Three little words many adult daughters have told a parent just before they slammed a door or hung up a phone. Adult sons simply stop calling altogether, leaving us to wonder what in the world we did wrong. Somebody should have given us the bad news: adult children can be mean.

Though my daughter never screamed caustic words at me, her heart belonged to my husband alone. Anna, like many young women, was a self-proclaimed daddy's girl. Throughout her life, he'd been her go-to parent. "I'm just like Dad," she would explain. "Besides, Nathan is your favorite."

Sadly, I was too distracted to hear Anna at the time. But the Lord, in his mercy, wrestled me out of my stupor shortly before she turned eighteen.

"Mom, for my eighteenth birthday . . . " The rest of my daughter's sentence sounded to me like an adult in a Charlie Brown special: *Wah wah wah wah wah.*

Anna spoke clearly enough, but I couldn't hear her. The upcoming reality of those last four words distracted me: "for her eighteenth birthday."

"Mom? Mom!" I looked up at my daughter. "I'm sorry. What? What were you saying?" She shook her head, and her eyes narrowed. "You weren't listening, were you?"[1]

Ironically, though we lament that our adult children don't listen to us, we might need to acknowledge the mountain of times that *we* haven't heard *them*. Like when my five-year-old son asked me to sign up to be his room mother. I hugged him and muttered something about having to work instead of seeking a way I could do it. Or the time ten-year-old Anna called from school saying she was sick. As a nurse, I knew she wasn't ill, so I told her to go back to class. But I did wonder why she was trying to get my attention. Did I ask her when she got home? No. How about when prom night ended at nine o'clock—way too early to be considered a lovely evening—and a stoic Anna said she was fine and headed to her room? I was slightly relieved. I had no right to be mad when her dad went to check on her, listened to her disappointments, and again emerged as Anna's parent-who-understands-me.

A Greater Offense

All three of these scenarios are clear failings from my past. Yes, they were sins against my children, but ultimately, they were sins against God. When David sinned against Bathsheba and Nathan confronted him, David recorded his repentance in Psalm 51: "Against

---

1   This introductory story was previously published in Gaye Clark and Anna Clark Wiggins, "9 Things Adult Daughters Want Their Mothers to Know," Gospel Coalition, May 8, 2015, https://www.thegospelcoalition.org/. Used by permission.

you, you only, have I sinned and done what is evil in your sight, so that you may be justified in your words and blameless in your judgment" (v. 4). David was not saying he didn't sin against Bathsheba; sin of course mars our human relationships. He was saying that God alone is the ultimate judge.

When we fail our children, we must first confess our sins to God. We must foremost fear the damage to our relationship with God, as David did when he prayed, "Cast me not away from your presence, and take not your Holy Spirit from me" (Ps. 51:11). It stands to reason that the solution starts with repentance toward God. What does that look like? The Greek word for repentance is *metanoia*. *Meta* means "to change," and *noia* refers to "the mind." Repentance, then, is to change one's mind. We grow to hate the things God hates and love the things God loves. In other words, repentance is not a onetime event at conversion. Rather, it is an ongoing experience that continues for the rest of our lives.

Neither Hot nor Cold

Sometimes our sins are easier to see when we look back and revisit our past choices and behaviors. Sadly, we can't go back in time and undo those mistakes, but we can speak honestly about those choices and our blindness—even years later. We can ask forgiveness for what we see now but didn't see then. Further, we might ask ourselves, What sins am I blind to today that grieve God or my kids now?

The New Testament church in Laodicea had its own issue with seeing. Like many of our churches, Laodicea was wealthy, influential in the community, and lukewarm in their love toward God. In Revelation, Jesus said to them,

I know your works: you are neither cold nor hot. Would that you were either cold or hot! So, because you are lukewarm, and neither hot nor cold, I will spit you out of my mouth. For you say, I am rich, I have prospered, and I need nothing, not realizing that you are wretched, pitiable, poor, blind, and naked. (Rev. 3:15–17)

This self-sufficient church couldn't see their spiritual poverty. Their Jesus was a small god who they called on at mealtimes, the Sabbath, and other occasions when a spiritual bellhop was needed. But rarely did their hearts break for what broke his.

The verse "Behold, I stand at the door and knock," found later in this section (3:20), is often thought of evangelistically, but in the context of Revelation 3, Jesus is still addressing the church in Laodicea. Preaching on this passage, John Piper noted,

This verse can be applied (without damage, I think) to an unbeliever (as we often use it), but that is not its purpose here. It is addressed to lukewarm Christians who think they have need of nothing more of Christ. It is addressed to churchgoers who do not enjoy the riches of Christ or the garments of Christ or the medicine of Christ because they keep the door shut to the inner room of their lives. All the dealings they have with Christ are businesslike lukewarm dealings with a salesman on the porch.[2]

Have you seen the famous Sunday school painting of Revelation 3:20? Some versions show an anemic Jesus standing outside

2 John Piper, "How to Buy Gold When You're Broke," Desiring God, January 2, 1983, https://www.desiringgod.org/.

a fashionable door, knocking. He too seems to be pleading for someone to let him in. It's quite different from the first picture that depicted this passage. The original painting was entitled *The Light of the World* by William Holman Hunt. It was an allegorical work, each detail ripe with meaning. Hunt depicted a weathered door with vines and trees covering the outside. No one had touched it in years. The door had no handle, so it had to be opened from the inside. This door represented an obstinately shut mind. There, a triumphant Jesus stood, wearing a crown, yet humbly knocking.

We must be careful not to read too much into this. Technically, no one can respond to God without him first working in them. Nonetheless, there is a point to see here. Jesus knows what it feels like to be marginalized, disrespected, and, as Piper put it, to be treated with "businesslike lukewarm dealings."

Lukewarm? Some of us have adult kids who are ice-cold. Your heart aches with each disrespectful tone, ignored birthday, and cruel comeback to an innocent question. They keep you at a distance, never letting you in—even if they live under the same roof with you. Yet when we ache over our kids' coldness toward us, do we consider our own coldness toward God?

When was the last time you wept over your sin? What habit, desire, or agenda has God recently challenged you to surrender to him? When was the last time you actively sought the Lord and asked him to open your eyes to unconfessed or unrepented sin in your life? These kinds of spiritual encounters and practices can greatly affect your relationship with your adult child because your offenses toward God affect not only your walk with him but others too. When our hearts ache over the behavior of our adult children, do we remember that we may have negative behaviors that they can clearly see and we cannot?

Godly Sorrow versus Worldly Sorrow

The media frequently features celebrities caught in embarrassing sins, reading statements where they pledge to take responsibility for their actions. They are careful never to name the behavior as sin and even more careful never to define what responsibility would look like going forward. This false repentance falls flat, not only with God but with the people they have harmed. It is what the Bible calls worldly grief. Anyone can feel bad about something they did, but not everyone truly repents. True repentance leads to changed behavior.

An adult daughter—we will call her Miranda—listened to a similar shallow apology from her mother that never named her mother's sin nor defined her future actions in measurable terms. Miranda wasn't having it. "Are you sorry, Mom, or are you repentant? Repentance names names."

Kevin DeYoung, senior pastor of Christ Covenant Church in Matthews, North Carolina, and father of nine children writes,

> Worldly grief is not good grief. It leads to death. Because worldly grief does not allow us to see our offensiveness to God, we don't deal with our sin in a vertical direction. And therefore, we don't get forgiveness from God, the lack of which leads to spiritual death. Worldly grief deals with symptoms not with the disease. Worldly grief produces despair, bitterness, and depression because it focuses on regret for the past (which can't be changed) or the present consequences (which

we can't fully avoid) instead of personal sinfulness (which can always be forgiven).[3]

It's easy to apologize but not truly repent when we're suffering the consequences of our sin. Worldly grief is feeling bad because we're suffering, not because our sin displeases a holy God. It then follows that our adult children may interpret an apology we offer them as us feeling regret not for the pain they experienced but for the consequences we are personally suffering from.

Eventually, being in denial of our spiritual state can even affect our physical well-being. A medical physician at the hospital I worked at once told me that half of what he sees in his office aren't medical conditions but spiritual ones—guilt and shame over unconfessed sin.

The apostle Paul spoke on this theme in his letters. In 2 Corinthians 7, he noted that worldly grief produces death but godly grief produces life. The emotional suffering the Corinthians endured because of godly grief was temporary. However, their salvation would be eternal.

> For even if I made you grieve with my letter, I do not regret it—though I did regret it, for I see that that letter grieved you, though only for a while. As it is, I rejoice, not because you were grieved, but because you were grieved into repenting. For you felt a godly grief, so that you suffered no loss through us. For godly grief produces a repentance that leads to salvation without regret, whereas worldly grief produces death. (2 Cor. 7:8–10)

3 Kevin DeYoung, "Worldly Grief," *The Gospel Coalition* (blog), June 1, 2010, https://www.thegospelcoalition.org/.

Yet, the Corinthians did not only weep. Look at verse 11: "For see what earnestness this godly grief has produced in you, but also what eagerness to clear yourselves, what indignation, what fear, what longing, what zeal, what punishment!" The Corinthians' repentance led them to a deeper devotion to God and, as the rest of the chapter infers, to one another.

Likewise, as we walk in a more loving relationship with our Lord, godly grief will lead us to repentance as well as a deeper awareness of our sins. Repentance toward God will guide us to speak to family and friends whom we have wronged and ask their forgiveness as well. Part of building a better relationship with your adult children, difficult as it may be, is to prayerfully ask God to reveal any area where you may need to ask for their forgiveness. This may also involve asking them to share other ways you may have wronged them.

As parents, we may fail to understand many things our children see as neglectful or even hurtful. Our shared memories can look different through their eyes. Anna's and Nathan's memories of several incidents in our past are distinct from mine, and it's been helpful to ask them, How did you experience that day?

It's important to ask our kids how we've hurt them—and in a way that allows them to be honest. Sin has a deceitful quality to it (Jer. 17:9), and it can seem exponential when we interact with our kids. We can have higher expectations of our children than we do of others, and when we feel betrayed by them, we may wait for them to come to us and apologize. Our children may be oblivious of any wrongdoing, or they may feel that they have been wronged in some way. Still, even if they pick up on your displeasure they may opt to ignore you. Satan rejoices at the stalemate. You may have suffered much from your children, but as "far as it depends on you," be at peace with them (Rom. 12:18). It's up to you to set the example and take the lead in repentance.

Often when women speak of listening, they are referring to something deeper than just hearing words. They want to be understood. One of the few studies on mother and adult daughter relationships notes that most daughters (90 percent) stated that their mothers listen to them, yet less than half (43 percent) reported that they felt understood by their mothers.[4]

Part one of ensuring your adult child feels understood is being willing to see yourself through their eyes—without defense, excuse, or even a plausible explanation. Ask the Lord to give you the strength to hear and understand their words, even if they are painful. Imagine what your child feels and suspend your feelings while doing so. Ask the Lord to give you grace to offer them a loving response. Don't let it be said of you, "I never heard my parents apologize to me."

Inviting your child's rebuke is not for the faint of heart, to be sure. If you or your adult child has a history of trauma, past abuse, or mental illness, you would be wise to seek support from a Christian counselor before having this conversation. You might seek out a counselor even if you do not have a history of trauma just because you feel the need for additional insight.

Perhaps your child has much he needs to confess as well. Nevertheless, parents ought to be the lead repenters in this relationship. Read what Paul says in Ephesians: "Be kind to one another, tenderhearted, forgiving one another, as God in Christ forgave

4   Maghboeba Mosavel, Christian Simon, and Debbie Van Stade, "The Mother–Daughter Relationship: What Is Its Potential as a Locus for Health Promotion?," *Health Care Women International* 27, no. 7 (August 2006): 646–64.

you" (4:32). Who wouldn't want to describe their relationship with their child as kind and tenderhearted? But the third word, "forgiving," presumes that there is a confession of sin.

When I asked my eighteen-year-old daughter to share her frustrations with me, one of the things she rightly brought up was my constant distraction: "I never feel like I have your full attention. You are always scrolling on your phone when I talk to you."

She had a point. What seemed like multitasking to me looked to my daughter like a mom who cared about everything else but her. No excuses or whatabouts would move us forward. I asked for her forgiveness and made a conscious effort to put my phone away when we spoke. At times, it led to Anna grinning and extending her hand with an unspoken, "Hand me that phone, missy!" She understood that I cared enough to change my behavior. As a mother of toddlers now, Anna is far more conscious of how her phone can create a distraction between her and her children than I was when raising her.

If a conversation like this one leads you to make an apology, remember that quality counts. I know a parent who, when apologizing to her children, does two additional things. First, she asks God to show her a concrete way, if possible, to offer restitution. For example, if she broke a promise that involved giving her time (like taking her kids to a concert), restitution might include taking a day off to make it right. This demonstrated to her kids the difference between an empty-sounding "Gee, I'm sorry" and true repentance. Second, she would mark on her calendar to ask her kids in three weeks, How am I doing in this area? This let her kids know that what was important to them (to see a changed parent) was important to her. Because this mom often asked to see growth and maturity from her children, she also had the humility to demonstrate the same. This is what it looks like to fight beside instead of against your kids when opposing sin and unbelief.

Not Guilty

Apologizing for the sin we know we have is one thing, but what if your child brings up a fault you aren't guilty of? Perhaps he sees the situation incorrectly, judges you unfairly, or resents outcomes you had no control over. You can first hear him out and agree that the perceived wounds he expresses are painful. Say something like, "Yes, being disrespected hurts." Then make a few inquiries to ensure you fully understand his perspective.

However, take care not to slip in any defensive questions like, Didn't you realize I was doing the best I could at the time? If you still don't agree that you have wronged him, you would be wise to tell him, "Let me think and pray on this, honey." If he is a believer, ask him to pray for you.

You might also consider asking a godly friend (with your child's permission) to give you her perspective on the situation. Your friend should not be afraid to tell you when you are in the wrong. Additionally, depending on the seriousness of the accusation, it might be good for the two of you to sit down with a third party, such as a counselor or pastor. It may be that after these steps you still disagree with your adult child but, at the very least, he knows you haven't dismissed him and have taken his concerns seriously.

Forgiveness in Christ

On the other hand, maybe you're sincerely grieved by your sin against your child, you've confessed and asked for forgiveness, and the only response was "I'm over it" followed by a slammed door. Your heart breaks. When an adult child withholds forgiveness, run to Christ and look at yourself through his lens. As you do this, it may be important to also look at your sin from your adult child's perspective. Ask the Lord to grant you empathy to understand his hurt and pain. This can go a long way toward understanding why he finds forgiveness so difficult and why it may be months or even years, depending on the circumstances, before he finds forgiveness possible. Daniel Darling, author of *A Way with Words*, writes,

> Jesus' forgiveness of us is so outrageous, so overflowing that we can draw on it more than seventy times seven for our own deep hurts. Jesus is helping us here. He is telling us that all our forgiveness doesn't have to happen in a moment. He is telling us that in some ways, perhaps in smaller and smaller doses over time, the deepest hurts will always be with us. How often have you assumed you were over something only to discover that indeed you are not?[5]

When we need forgiveness, we ache for immediate assurance from those we've wronged. But depending on the circumstances and the maturity level of the people involved, human forgiveness may need to be a long process, not a onetime event. Give your child time to build trust, and in the meantime, pray that the Lord would ultimately heal the rift between you. Look to your Savior and not to your child. Jesus alone will be your ultimate comfort.

5   Daniel Darling, "The Rhythm of Forgiveness and Repentance," *Daniel Darling* (blog), April 23, 2013, https://danieldarling.com/.

The assurance of Christ's love and the awareness of his presence proved vital in my relationship with Anna. Ultimately, it was the Lord who saved our relationship. Three years after my prom night fail, Anna and I would need to lean hard on one another as we faced the loss of the man we both loved, her father and my husband, Jim. After recieving his grim prognosis, I remember thinking, Who will walk my daughter down the aisle?

Later that night, I climbed the stairs to Anna's room. She looked at me for a moment, her green eyes shining. "I'm fine," she lied. Sometimes the Lord grants us do-overs. This was mine.

"No. No, you're not." I plopped down beside her and slipped my hand in hers as she laid her head on my shoulder. "Right now, neither am I. But one day, we will be. By God's grace, we will be."

Our children don't always welcome our redemptive revisions for past mistakes. And even when they do, reconciliation can be slow. Three years had passed since I missed my daughter's pain on prom night. What was worse, I now felt utterly helpless to comfort her. Yet, Anna didn't need to see a strong mom at this moment—she needed one who could fall apart in the arms of Jesus and invite her to do the same.

One of the most shattering realizations we parents must face is that what our kids need most isn't us but Christ. Our job is to point them to him. It is an ironic God blessing that we do this best when we're at our weakest.

Discussion Questions

1. Think back to a time when you realized that your child was advancing quickly to the realm of adulthood. How did it make you feel?

2. The church at Laodicea was charged with being lukewarm and downright blind to their true spiritual state. They believed they were rich when, in fact, they were blind and poor. How are we blind to our sins, and in what ways can that affect our adult children?

3. Sometimes offering an apology can be tricky. A good way to practice this is to think of someone who owes you an apology and imagine receiving a letter from them. What would you need it to say? Write that letter and look carefully at the key elements. Just as important, what should not be included in the apology?

4. What does our relationship with God have to do with our relationship with our adult children?

5. What is the key difference between godly grief and worldly sorrow? How does the latter negatively affect our relationships?

6. How should we proceed when an adult child accuses us of something we don't feel we are guilty of?

7. Look at Psalm 51, which is written by David during a time of deep conviction of sin. What gives David confidence to approach God and ask for forgiveness (vv. 1–3)? What are the effects of his sin (vv. 2–3)? Where is the turning point in the psalm? What gives David renewed hope? What is the great reversal (v. 8)?

3

Grace

AN ONLINE QUESTION AND ANSWER forum asked its readers, "Are you proud of what your adult children have grown up to be?"[1] The question received mixed responses. Among them was a father who said, "I am extremely disappointed in my daughter." She's "a beautiful, fit, tan brunette girl" who grew up in a loving home and was popular. At one time, Mom and Dad were proud of their caring daughter. Then she "got a tattoo on her forearms the day she turned eighteen."

"My wife and I were outraged," the father said. The problem? Her parents couldn't believe she would do that without consulting them. Dad said she got more tattoos in college and became sexually promiscuous. "I knew this was leading to dangerous roads for my daughter. I tried talking to her about it and she seemed like she understood my concern," he said.

---

1 "Are You Proud or Embarrassed of What Your Adult Children Have Grown Up To Be?," Quora, accessed August 16, 2022, https://www.quora.com/. All quotations in this section are from this source.

But a few weeks later, his son texted him. The son's friends had seen the daughter in a college porn video. Dad freaked out. "My wife and I called her and asked what was going on," he said. She confirmed his fears, saying they'd paired her with a "hot" guy. Dad got angry and told his daughter she couldn't come home.

Time has passed, she's now engaged to someone her parents haven't met, and Dad hasn't spoken to her in three months. He says, "Am I overreacting? Should I invite her and her fiancé back home?"

It's understandable to feel shame, betrayal, and anger when our adult children disappoint or humiliate us. Jesus knows how betrayal and humiliation feel. He suffered those things for our sake when we were unrepentant sinners (Rom. 5:8). But it wasn't a voice of wrath that stirred our hearts to conviction—it was his costly love. Christ forgave us much and at a great price. Knowing this can help us respond thoughtfully rather than reactively when we see our children sin.

Christ's Humiliation

On the night Jesus was betrayed, Peter, James, and John succumbed to weariness and fell asleep. Jesus prayed in the garden alone, "Father, if you are willing, remove this cup from me. Nevertheless, not my will, but yours, be done" (Luke 22:42). The Father's answer came as Judas approached with a mob and identified Jesus with a kiss. The disciples scattered, but Peter followed at a distance, only to deny knowing Jesus shortly after (22:60).

Even though Pilate believed Jesus was innocent, he bowed to the will of a bloodthirsty mob who shouted, "Crucify, crucify him!" (23:21). Where were those who just days before proclaimed, "Blessed is the King who comes in the name of the Lord"? (19:38).

Even in all this, Jesus prayed, "Father, forgive them, for they know not what they do" (23:34).

While the crowd mocked and spit on him, nails pierced his hands and feet. The crown of thorns stabbed his head as it pressed against the wood. The soldiers shouted, "If you are the King of the Jews, save yourself!" (23:37). If they only knew. Jesus faced one of the most horrible executions known to humanity—alone. But to say Jesus died for our sins doesn't tell the half of what he did for us. Jeremy Ward, head of the physiology department at King's College, London, explains, "Crucifixion was a method of torture—not just putting to death. It was a particularly cruel and unusual form of disposing of people."[2]

Our Humiliation

Consider how deeply wronged and humiliated your Savior was for your sake. Jesus understood what it was like to endure harm, abandonment, betrayal, and misunderstanding from family and friends. Yet he did not withhold his love based on their behavior; he didn't say, "I'm over it. I'm done." His example should inform the way we relate to our adult children. Remembering the cost of your salvation may not transform your adult son or daughter, but it can change you.

Are you willing to endure humiliation for the well-being of an adult child, even an unrighteous one? Are you willing to suffer injustice for the sake of someone you love? Is that not what Christ did for us? Luke 15 tells a story of a father whose adult sons wronged and humiliated him. This good and loving father

2   "How Was a Crucifixion Performed?," Bible Reading Archeology, August 28, 2018, https://biblereadingarcheology.com/.

suffered with sons who didn't love him. It should comfort parents to know that struggles with adult children aren't necessarily the result of bad parenting.

Jesus begins his parable by saying "there was a man who had two sons. And the younger of them said to his father, 'Father, give me the share of property that is coming to me'" (Luke 15:11–12). In the Greco-Roman world, sons would not receive an inheritance until their parents had died. A father could divide his property, but even if he did this, he still had control over it. In Jesus's parable, the younger son demanded both property and control. He wanted his father's possessions but not a relationship with him. Kenneth E. Bailey explains that the son did not ask for his inheritance because

> to accept one's "inheritance" involves acceptance of leadership responsibility in the family clan. The recipient is duty bound to administer property and solve family quarrels. He must defend the honor of the family against all comers (even with his life, if necessary). He pledges himself to increase the clan's wealth and represent them nobly at village functions (such as weddings, feasts, and funerals). He must "build" the house of his father. But this is specifically what the younger son does not want and does not ask for. He wants the money![3]

Many parents can relate. An adult child may feel entitled to the benefits of your labors without the responsibilities that come with them, making you feel like nothing more than an ATM.

3   Kenneth E. Bailey, *The Cross and the Prodigal: Luke 15 Through the Eyes of Middle Eastern Peasants*, 2nd ed. (Downers Grove, IL: InterVarsity, 2005), 43.

But do we treat God the same way? When I took a hard look at my prayer life, I noticed how often I asked God to do something for me instead of thanking him for what he had already accomplished. I had a habit of praying for what worried me but not what concerned God. How often are we content to be in his presence without seeking anything from him? If you think your adult children may be struggling with feelings of entitlement, perhaps it is an opportunity to bring your frustration to the Lord. Ask him to help you seek him not for what he can give you but for who he is.

Suffering Grace

So what did the father in the parable say to his younger son who had broken his heart? He had every right to disown his child. Such action would have provided little hope for reconciliation, but it would have spared him further humiliation. Yet, instead of doing this, he broke every parenting tip on the planet: he answered his son's entitled request in the affirmative. In doing so, he chose to suffer. Jesus says, "Not many days later, the younger son gathered all he had and took a journey into a far country, and there he squandered his property in reckless living" (15:13).

The younger son wasted no time liquidating the nonmonetary assets.[4] He may have received land or treasures the father had hoped would stay in the family for generations. Now, all gone. Sold on the auction block to the highest bidder—friends, neighbors, and even enemies. The father and his family could have become the subject of town gossip. How could he let his son just walk all over him like that?

4   Wayne Grudem and Thomas R. Schreiner, study notes for the Gospel of Luke in the *ESV Study Bible* (Wheaton, IL: Crossway, 2016), 2154.

Jesus continues, saying that when the son

> had spent everything, a severe famine arose in that country, and he began to be in need. So he went and hired himself out to one of the citizens of that country, who sent him into his fields to feed pigs. And he was longing to be fed with the pods that the pigs ate, and no one gave him anything. (15:14–16)

God used the heat of these circumstances to create the desperation the younger son experienced. He was hungry—so hungry that pig slop looked appetizing. Unfortunately for this younger son, humans couldn't survive on these pods.[5] Still, he didn't head home yet. He might have dreaded the thought of being under the thumb of both his dad and his older brother. So he hunkered down a bit longer.

But his father was waiting—and suffering—too. How long do you wait for a child to return? Many parents of adult children are in a difficult time of watching and praying. Your adult daughter may live with an abusive boyfriend who won't let her out of his sight. Drugs might consume your adult son so that he can no longer live under your roof and you have no idea where he sleeps at night. They live in a far-off country in utter despair. You wonder why they don't come home. You cry out, "How long, O Lord?" (Ps. 13:1).

I knew parents who prayed for their estranged son for over fifteen years before he bowed the knee to Christ. When he did, the entire church shared their joy! We don't know how long the father in Jesus's

---

5   According to Kenneth Bailey, "The word for 'pods' is *keration*, which may refer to the seed pods of the carob tree (*Ceratonia siliqua*), a variety of locust or acacia. A human cannot survive on the pods themselves. Pigs can." Bailey, *The Cross and the Prodigal*, 58.

parable waited, but we do know that waiting is the most difficult part for parents who endure rejected love. Keep praying. Is anything too difficult for God? Rarely are our adult children convinced to make the journey toward home because of an eloquent speech we gave them or our brilliant counter to one of their accusations. After exhausting our plans and sermons, the still, small voice that God may choose to use is often the heat of a circumstance.

Compassionate Grace

In God's timing, the younger son of Jesus's parable

> came to himself, he said, "How many of my father's hired servants have more than enough bread, but I perish here with hunger! I will arise and go to my father, and I will say to him, 'Father, I have sinned against heaven and before you. I am no longer worthy to be called your son. Treat me as one of your hired servants.'" (Luke 15:17–19)

It was certainly progress to recognize his situation was dire. But here's the million-dollar question: Did this boy experience repentance or was he just desperate for relief? He prepared a confession without specifics and made plans to get out of the pigsty. "Father, I have sinned against heaven and before you" comes straight out of Pharaoh's playbook: "I have sinned against the LORD your God, and against you" (Ex. 10:16). Pharaoh feigned repentance to manipulate Moses and the Israelites.

This younger son wanted to strike a deal with Dad so he could *work* his way out of his sin, not accept grace. He thought the issue was the money—pay it back, and everything would be fine. But it was much deeper than that for his dad, wasn't it? The broken relationship was lost on the son. And did this younger son really think he could learn a trade, earn money, and repay his debt? Did he have any clue about the amount he truly owed?

Given his crimes, he should have offered himself up as a slave. He certainly deserved to be one. But he didn't do this—I mean, slaves don't get paid, right? Our younger son doesn't get it.

Have your adult children come to you with promises you know they cannot keep? How would you respond? The father in the parable did the following: "While [his son] was still a long way off, his father saw him and felt compassion, and ran and embraced him and kissed him" (Luke 15:20).

After all the wounds this boy had inflicted upon his dad, the father felt compassion! Wasn't he angry, even a little? Jesus doesn't say, but there can be no doubt, given the depth of this father's love, that his son had caused the father deep suffering.

We can feel grief and lament the pain of broken relationships. When our adult children sin against us, we can offer them the kindness of speaking the truth in love. But we should not grow bitter, sulk, and stay angry at God or our adult children. To do this, we need godly friends in our lives, walking with us to help us know when we've strayed from lament and grief and into bitterness.

Amazing Grace

In Jesus's parable, the father wasn't the only person who might have been angry. This son would have stirred up the wrath of the entire town[6] and risked an angry mob greeting him when

6   Bailey, *The Cross and the Prodigal*, 66.

he returned. But rather than see his son face the humiliation he rightly deserved, this father did something that was considered undignified for someone his age and stature in his culture: he picked up his garment and ran. After all he had suffered, this dad came down from his home and took his son's shame by running to meet the lad ahead of the village's would-be mockers. He ran to the rescue.

This contrasts with what we often read on social media websites when frustrated parents "discipline" their teens and young adults by posting their misdeeds and subsequent punishments. These parents may have won the immediate battle, but I assure you, the war they are fighting will only become more entrenched. What is most often on display on these public posts isn't just the child's misdeeds but the sinful pride of the parent eager to obtain a commendation for disciplining well.

Teasing our kids, though not rising to the offense of posting their wrongs to social media, can also be hurtful. I had a habit of doing this until my children had the courage to confront me. They gave me the opportunity to apologize and repair our relationship. Looking back, I now see that this too was a form of shame, and it was not funny at all.

When God confronts us with our sin, he does so with love. It is speaking the truth in love, not shaming, that brings repentance. As Romans 2:4 says, "Or do you presume on the riches of his kindness and forbearance and patience, not knowing that God's *kindness* is meant to lead you to repentance?"

I have listened to brokenhearted, anguished young adults whose parents had clearly communicated to them the wrath of God (they called it "holding them accountable") yet failed to express the undying, unconditional love of God. This omission may be because their parents had never fully experienced the love of God firsthand. Or it could be that their anger consumed them. Not only do their children feel they can't go home again, but they also do not believe God loves them. Truth without love is a poison that will infect these young hearts. And when this happens, heaven weeps. If we passionately give our adult children the truth, we need that truth to be foremost that God saves sinners because he loves them. They can quote us chapter and verse on God's wrath; Satan has made certain of that.

In Jesus's parable, he focused on love without ignoring sin. He continued,

And the son said to him, "Father, I have sinned against heaven and before you. I am no longer worthy to be called your son." But the father said to his servants, "Bring quickly the best robe, and put it on him, and put a ring on his hand, and shoes on his feet. And bring the fattened calf and kill it, and let us eat and celebrate. For this my son was dead, and is alive again; he was lost, and is found." And they began to celebrate. (Luke 15:21–24)

The father's love unraveled the younger son's plan. He dropped the hired servant scheme and faced whatever consequences his loving father willed. And his father willed a glorious celebration!

Exasperating Grace

Though one son surrendered, this father had yet another son to face. Isn't that the way of parenting sometimes? The parable says,

Now his older son was in the field, and as he came and drew near to the house, he heard music and dancing. And he called one of the servants and asked what these things meant. And he said to him, "Your brother has come, and your father has killed the fattened calf, because he has received him back safe and sound." But he was angry and refused to go in. His father came out and entreated him. (15:25–28)

We love to speak fondly of grace, how much we love it, need it—especially when we are its recipients. But when called to extend grace, well, that's another thing entirely. Grace doesn't always feel amazing. Sometimes it's downright exasperating. It's more than enough to get on a Pharisee's nerves. For the second time in the same day, the father bore the humiliation of dealing with a son's shameful behavior. This time, it was the elder son.

The father's guests would have seen this son's adult tantrum outside the home as a grave insult to his dad. The father had every right to discipline him sharply, but that would have deepened the divide between them. He could have ignored his son's behavior and waited to deal with him until after his guests left, but that would have enabled his older son to take greater liberties.

Instead, the father left his guests in a public manner and tenderly pled with his son for genuine restoration. The older son professed to be the better son. After all, he had kept the law and wanted his reward. He couldn't see how much he had in common with his younger brother.

The older son made his case to his dad: " Look, these many years I have served you, and I never disobeyed your command, yet you never gave me a young goat, that I might celebrate with my friends.

But when this son of yours came, who has devoured your property with prostitutes, you killed the fattened calf for him!" (15:29–30).

"I have served you, and I never disobeyed your command." Really? *Never?* This is reminiscent of the rich ruler who told Jesus, "All these [laws] I have kept from my youth" (18:21). The older son, even if he managed perfect obedience at home, failed in his duty to the family. He had a duty to find the younger son and bring him home.[7]

Thus, the older son's loyalty claim was bogus. He didn't even address his father by name. He also referred to his brother as "this son of yours." That doesn't sound like loyalty. For this older son, fulfilling his duty meant keeping a list of sins he didn't commit, and he failed to see the proactive obligations he owed his father because those actions required love. He failed to be faithful because he failed to love. "You *never* gave me a young goat, that I might celebrate with my friends" infers that the father gave him nothing—ever. In truth, his father had divided the inheritance when the younger son had left, and the older son also received his share (15:12).

When the sins of those we love (like an adult child) make us angry—and understandably so—we should acknowledge our need for a Savior instead of pointing to a false record of sinless perfection. Otherwise, we can be more like the older son than we realize. Jesus's response to this attitude is, "Son, you are always with me, and all that is mine is yours. It was fitting to celebrate and be glad, for this your brother was dead, and is alive; he was lost, and is found" (15:31–32).

---

7 Bailey, *The Cross and the Prodigal*, 45.

Empowering Grace

This father absorbed tremendous pain and suffering to love these two men, his sons, for years. If you've ever walked with someone through suffering, this question inevitably comes up: How do you endure? Days after my husband died, I placed 2 Corinthians 12:9 on my bedroom wall, where I'd see it each morning. It reads, "[Jesus] said to me, 'My grace is sufficient for you, for my power is made perfect in weakness.' Therefore I will boast all the more gladly of my weaknesses, so that the power of Christ may rest upon me." This was my reminder to get out of bed—because some days I didn't feel like it. In reading that verse day after day, it became apparent that grace was not only unmerited salvation. Grace was also an unmerited power, given by God, to enable us to endure suffering.

If you are heartbroken over your relationship with your child, mistakes you've made, or words you cannot take back, remember the cross, and remember that three days after that grisly death, our Savior rose from the grave to save you and to continue saving you. You can boldly approach the throne of the one who endured our shame. He understands every ache and pain you have suffered and every tear you have shed. Imagine him as your father, who, when he sees you in the distance, runs to you. He will equip you not only to fight your battles but also to flourish, "for we do not have a high priest who is unable to sympathize with our weaknesses, but one who in every respect has been tempted as we are, yet without sin. Let us then with confidence draw near to the throne of grace, that we may receive mercy and find grace to help in time of need" (Heb. 4:15–16).

Discussion Questions

1. In what ways do the older and younger brothers of Jesus's parable, though different externally, have similar spiritual needs? Did the father of these two sons love them equally? Why or why not?

2. Do your adult children walk confidently in your love or do they believe your love is conditional? Do you have the courage to discuss this topic with them and listen to their response without being defensive?

3. In what ways have you corrected your adult children with shame?

4. Have you thought deeply about how much your Savior loves you? How does reflecting on the cross inform your response to your adult children?

5. Grace is not just unmerited salvation but also empowerment to do what God has called us to, including enduring suffering. In what ways can grace strengthen you today?

4

Hope

MISTY SMITH RECALLS the bondage that drugs had on her life: "I used to wake up and my prayers went something like this: 'Really? Another day, *really*?' I kept hoping I would die, but every day I would wake up to the disappointment that I was still breathing."

For Misty, there seemed to be no way out. Then police slapped handcuffs on her. The judge gave her a choice: serve eight years in prison or go to drug rehab. She opted for the latter.

"At first I didn't want to get clean; I just didn't want to go to jail," Misty said. "I was so strung out on drugs; I didn't have any feelings about anything or anyone. All I cared about was getting the next fix."

But as the drugs wore off, her mind began to think, and her heart began to feel. She thought about her two girls, Brittiany and Asia, who had been removed from her home years ago and placed in the care of other family members because of her drug habit. Misty began to weep. She brushed back her tears, saying "To think who I gave up for that load of garbage."

She asked her sponsor about meeting with the girls to start the process of reconciliation. Would they even speak with her, let alone want a relationship with her? Was it too much to hope for?

An Anchor in the Storm

The writer of Hebrews tells us, "Now faith is the assurance of things hoped for, the conviction of things not seen" (Heb. 11:1). Assurance—this isn't a word we use to describe an iffy circumstance. One thing we can be sure of is our God, even though we do not see him. In all our wishes and hopes with our adult children, we must keep in mind the one great hope: our Savior, who has promised to never leave us nor forsake us, no matter what trial we face.

Hebrews 6 says, "We have this as a sure and steadfast anchor of the soul, a hope that enters into the inner place behind the curtain, where Jesus has gone as a forerunner on our behalf, having become a high priest forever after the order of Melchizedek" (6:19–20). What is this hope? It is in the person and saving work of Christ, the great high priest.

Note the metaphor used in this passage: "anchor of the soul." Anchors can stabilize the mightiest of ships by using their weight to hold a vessel in place. The anchor not only prevents the ship from being washed out to sea but also has drag mechanisms to keep the ship stable and steady during a violent storm. This prevents the sea winds and waves from slamming the bow, flooding the deck, and potentially sinking the ship. As the famous hymn says, "In every high and stormy gale, my anchor holds within the veil."[1] Our God will keep us, steady us, and not allow us to drown beneath the waves.

---

1   Edward Mote, "My Hope Is Built on Nothing Less" (1834).

Back to our story on Misty. Asia agreed to meet her mom, but Brittiany took some persuading. Sometimes when parents meet with adult children, the former have no idea what has caused the divide between them. But when the big day came for Misty to meet with her adult daughters, she didn't need to rack her brain to search for what she had done to cause the rift—she knew. The condemnation she placed on herself alone could have crushed her, never mind what she expected to hear from her daughters. "I was waiting for them to throw knives at me, you know? I deserved it. I totally deserved it. In some ways, it would have helped, but then I realized there's no way to pay for what I'd done—and what I did not do."

Moms and dads need a Savior every bit as much as their adult children, whether their sin is as serious as Misty's or not. Misty had begun a journey that precluded using drugs to escape from her pain and suffering. In reaching out to reconcile with her adult daughters, she chose to face the demons of her past, acknowledge the wrong she had done, and risk her daughters' ultimate rejection. In order to reconcile, she chose suffering.

Suffering Leads to Hope

The apostle Paul wrote that if you're a Christian, you're going to suffer. He anticipated the next question we would ask when we encounter suffering: Is it worth it?

Paul wrote,

> The Spirit himself bears witness with our spirit that we are children of God, and if children, then heirs—heirs of God and fellow heirs with Christ, provided we suffer with him in order that we may also be glorified with him. For I consider that the

sufferings of this present time are not worth comparing with the glory that is to be revealed to us. (Rom. 8:16–18)

His answer to the question "Is it worth it?" is a resounding, absolute, no-holds-barred "Yes!" Yes—because Christ is worth it. Our hope is not in our circumstances or our friends and family. We place our hope in Christ alone, who promises never to leave or forsake us.

In Christ, whatever we have suffered has no comparison to the glories we will experience in the future. Considering the atrocities some have endured, this is an astounding claim. Think back to what Paul endured and what so many suffered through wars, slavery, every sort of injustice, human oppression, and natural disasters—and what your family may have endured. Paul, are you telling us there is no comparison? Yes. Rather than vanquish hope, our trials propel us toward hope.

Read what Paul said in an earlier passage:

Therefore, since we have been justified by faith, we have peace with God through our Lord Jesus Christ. Through him we have also obtained access by faith into this grace in which we stand, and we rejoice in hope of the glory of God. Not only that, but we rejoice in our sufferings, knowing that suffering produces endurance, and endurance produces character, and character produces hope, and hope does not put us to shame, because God's love has been poured into our hearts through the Holy Spirit who has been given to us. (Rom. 5:1–5)

How can we have hope when faced with disappointment? By knowing that the finished work of Christ secured our peace with God through faith and granted us access to our heavenly Father. When trials come, we can run to him, as only any true child would, for something only he can give—grace, matchless grace.

When you listen to your adult children tell you how your drug habit caused them years of unspeakable pain, you desperately need that kind of grace. When you realize you have squandered years of their childhood, you need that kind of grace. When you have no clue what you have done to create a chasm between you and your adult child, you need that kind of grace. When you listen to your child spout off a list of wrongs you are not guilty of just to get a conversation started, you need that kind of grace. As parents, we are often faced with tasks that are too big for us to endure. That is yet another merciful reminder that we still need a Savior.

And, as Paul said, our suffering is not all for nothing. God will use it to create endurance (or as some translations call it, "perseverance"), which will produce character and then hope. In other words, our suffering has a purpose. God uses it to transform us into the image of Christ. This is true even when our suffering is the result of our sin (and its consequences) amid repentance. While we endure the process, God draws near to us. Psalm 56:8 says God counts our "tossings" and saves our tears in a bottle. He never wastes our pain. Not one drop.

But our transformation doesn't happen overnight. Praise God for his patience with us and for the kind people he sends our way to bear with us when we suffer. May we have eyes to see them. Let's now look at a parent in Scripture who found herself in great pain and the adult daughter God used to help her.

Less than Ideal

Naomi is one of the most honest characters in Scripture when it comes to pain. It's instructive to see her interaction with her adult daughter-in-law Ruth while these two women walked through insurmountable grief.

Naomi, her husband, and their two sons had moved to Moab to avoid a famine (Ruth 1:2). Fast forward to when her sons grew up, and Naomi has found herself a widow and her sons married to Moabite women. Not the ideal situation for a devoted Jewish parent.

All of us have some aspect of less-than-ideal in our families. It might be sin, such as an adult child living with someone before marriage. It may be the consequences of another's sin: your adult daughter struggling to make ends meet as a single parent after her husband left her for another woman. Or perhaps we see our situation—changing careers or moving to another state—as less than ideal simply because of our own preferences.

Parents who are estranged from their adult children often look back at their earlier parenting years searching for answers to the why question. Could it be their fault? Mom's and dad's demanding careers meant they weren't at their son's baseball games or they missed other important milestones in his life, for example. Is it all coming back to bite them? When looking for answers, we need to seek the Lord, search the Scriptures, and if necessary, consult a friend, pastor, or elder. If these parents conclude that they have wronged their adult children, even if the wrong was years ago, they would do well to seek their adult child's forgiveness.

Sacrificial Love

When Naomi decided to return home, she discouraged her daughters-in-law from going with her. But Ruth clung to her. Ruth's words are famously repeated, sometimes taken out of context, but always admired:

> Do not urge me to leave you or to return from following you. For where you go I will go, and where you lodge I will lodge. Your people shall be my people, and your God my God. Where you die I will die, and there will I be buried. May the LORD do so to me and more also if anything but death parts me from you. (1:16–17)

Ruth put it all on the line. Naomi didn't press her further, nor did she acknowledge the sacrifice Ruth pledged to make. Ruth would give up everything and everyone she had known to be a companion for Naomi. Assuming Naomi's bleak forecast was accurate, Ruth could kiss any hope for remarriage goodbye. But none of this deterred her.

Blinded by Pain

Yet, we don't read one word of gratitude from Naomi. Grief and suffering can make us as prickly as a porcupine and blind us to the jewel that is our adult child. We might overlook their efforts to connect or be kind to us when we are drowning in pain. That was certainly my experience in the early days of being a widow. My daughter would make me a special breakfast or leave me a loving note with an encouraging verse, but I hardly acknowledged her presence. A good friend called me on it and said, "She's hurting, too, Gaye. But she's still trying to care for you. You can at least let her know you see her."

Pain can also cause us to become excessively critical of our adult children. Sometimes, we give our critique without encouragement. We might recall our own difficult childhood, compare it to the easy upbringing we think our children enjoyed, and wish for a better response from them than we have seen. But how can they have gratitude for something they haven't experienced? And have we not simply done for them what we were obligated to do as parents? Our unspoken desire for appreciation and admiration from our adult children can have us holding them to impossible standards and lying to ourselves that it is for their own good when, in reality, it is for us. Our words, though well-intentioned, don't bring them life. Instead, they vanquish hope.

One of the biggest reasons many adult children distance themselves from their parents is to flee the constant criticism. Parents might not have considered the proper time and place for their words. They also may not be aware of their adult child's true emotional state.

In a 2019 study published by the American Psychological Association, 71 percent of young adults between the ages of eighteen and twenty-five reported experiencing serious psychological distress or major depression. Forty-seven percent of young adults acknowledged having suicidal thoughts.[2] Many of our

2   Jean M. Twenge, A. Bell Cooper, Thomas E. Joiner, Mary E. Duffy, and Sarah G. Binau, "Age, Period, and Cohort Trends in Mood Disorder Indicators and Suicide-Related Outcomes in a Nationally Representative Dataset, 2005–17," *Journal of Abnormal Psychology* 128, no. 3 (2019): 185–99.

young adults are not okay. Among women between the ages of eighteen and twenty-five, the numbers grow even higher. If we are distracted, caught up in our own struggles (however legitimate), we will be as cold as I was to my daughter when her father died. We will not hear their pledge of love and devotion; we will miss it entirely. Worse, we won't hear their cries for help either, and this might lead to tragic consequences.

Our adult children will learn just as much about the God we profess by the way we respond to our own trials as they do from the lectures we give them. Fortunately, as we see in Naomi's story, God grants us grace.

Finding Something Positive

Ruth told her mother-in-law, "Your people shall be my people, and your God my God" (1:16). Isn't that remarkable? Naomi hadn't been the most winsome witness for the beauty of Jehovah. She'd charged him with being the reason for her misery, and Ruth was probably aware that Moab wasn't on the Lord's list of favored nations. Despite all this, Ruth signed up. She might have been drawn to a God who could be spoken to honestly and plainly, as Naomi had shown. You certainly would not have tried that with the pagan gods of Moab. Ruth also might have viewed Naomi's decision to return to Bethlehem as courageous. Thus, instead of focusing on Naomi's melancholy spirit, she found something positive to notice and support. Ruth locked arms with her silent, bitter mother-in-law and hoped it might help Naomi's stumbling faith and heal her heart.

We parents would do well to follow her example. Find something positive in your adult children even when they are in despair or when some negative personality trait is front and center. Focus on that positive aspect, reinforce it, and help them lean into it.

When I speak with young adults who have troubled relationships with their parents, I ask them how they believe their parents see them. The question can often spark pain in many of these kids. While they will acknowledge their parents told them they loved them, they felt such an overwhelming feeling of condemnation that it made it difficult for them to truly accept those words. Or, as one young man told me, "My dad loves me, but he doesn't *like* me. It makes me wonder if he'd rather have someone else be his son."

A Trustworthy Relative

In the story of Naomi, we see that she not only liked Ruth but had also formed a deep bond of trust with her over the years. After the two return to Israel, between that first load of groceries Ruth carried home and Naomi's plan to get Ruth married off to Boaz, there are precious few details. What *was* clear was that Naomi's plan required a bold move on Ruth's part—Ruth had to go to the threshing floor and lie at Boaz's feet, where only men were sleeping. However strange Naomi's plan may have sounded, Ruth responded with, "All that you say I will do" (3:5). No second-guessing the state of Naomi's mind; just genuine trust in Naomi's plan, which paid off. When Boaz woke up, Ruth asked him, "Spread the corners of your garment over me, since you are a redeemer" (3:9). In other words, "I am willing to marry you, if you'd be open to that."

Apparently, Ruth's respect for Naomi was forged long before loss invaded their lives. This speaks volumes of who Naomi was before their tragedy struck. She must have built a relationship with Ruth that could weather the kind of relational stress that loss and suffering often bring.

When life is going well with you and your adult children, are you building into that relationship so that it can endure hardship and suffering? Naomi might have done so with her daughters-in-law, despite their being Moabite women, and it led to amazing consequences. Ruth trusted Naomi's judgment so much that she dared to lay at Boaz's feet in the middle of the night, which led to a wedding, a child, provision for Naomi, and even the advent of our Lord.

A Reason to Hope

Ruth and Boaz had a son, Obed. After several begets, King David was born, and after several more begets, Christ Jesus, who came to save his people from their sins. Naomi's sorrow *had* mattered.

God isn't afraid of our anger, bitterness, and frustration as we struggle in our pain and suffering. He remains with us always. His love is everlasting. He brings kind souls—sometimes in-laws and adult children—to walk beside us in our pain. He is the ultimate source of hope.

On October 19, 2022, Brittiany posted on her Facebook page:

> My mom, Misty Smith was an addict and I swear she's one of the strongest people I know. It takes so much trust and confidence to not only admit you have a problem but ask for help and stick with it. My mom has taught me so many things, including hope, forgiveness, love, empathy and understanding. To my mom, I can't tell you how proud I am of you every day. I could never be as strong as you. *Thank you for never giving up*

trying to be in my life when I gave up on you. I can't imagine my life right now without you. You are my best friend.[3]

I asked Misty what it felt like to read those words so publicly proclaimed from the daughter who, for a long time, wouldn't meet with her at all. With her watery eyes shining, Misty shook her head. It was several moments before she could speak:

Undeserving. Grateful. Rehab encourages you to find a higher power. I always knew God was my higher power. Every single day I need God. I don't know what will hit me tomorrow. I will always need God. So now I have a new prayer. Now I wake up and say, "Thank you God for another day and for a reason to live."

Not every human reconciliation effort concludes with a happy ending. True hope cannot reside in an earthly reconciliation, however beautiful it may be. Misty Smith, though overjoyed to be reconciled with her adult daughters, cannot place her ultimate hope in them. That is a heavy burden they cannot bear. We are not promised tomorrow, and God forbid, if something were to happen to one of her girls, how would she weather the storm? It would depend on where she had placed her ultimate hope.

If you know anything of the pain of a severed relationship with someone you dearly love, remember that God knows that pain too. He chose to sacrifice his Son in order to reconcile us

---

3 Brittiany Lawton, Facebook, October 19, 2022, http://www.facebook.com.

to himself. Your pain may enable you to cherish the finished work of Christ with greater devotion because you know something of the Father's pain and the fellowship of his sufferings. His strength will stabilize and steady you and prevent the waves of pain from drowning you. Press on in hope and continue to pray, "for nothing will be impossible with God" (Luke 1:37).

Discussion Questions

1. Have you ever thought it was just too late to repair your relationship with your adult child? What was that situation like? Was it truly too late?

2. When you've struggled to know where to find hope, who or what helped you? Was there a particular passage of Scripture you found encouraging?

3. Can you see how God has worked in your less-than-ideal family? Has he changed your heart in the process? If so, how?

4. Naomi and her husband opted to leave the country when a famine hit Judah. Scripture notes they remained there for some time, which may not have been their initial intent. Have you ever made a decision like that, thinking, "This is just until something changes," only to later realize that a change never came? How did that go?

5. Has there been a time when you couldn't see the gift of your adult son or daughter because you were blinded by your own suffering or pain? Have you told them about that time and expressed gratitude for them?

6. Read Psalm 121, an encouragement for those traveling to Jerusalem to worship. According to verse 2, how does knowing that God is the maker of heaven and earth give us confidence that he can help us? Note the repetition of the word "keep" (which means to guard, watch over, or attend carefully to); what does this tell us about God's care for us? Verse 4 notes that God never sleeps; how might knowing this truth grant us greater assurance of God's care? While this psalm was originally for sojourners to Jerusalem, how might it apply to your circumstances today?

5

Church

ONE SUNDAY, WE LEFT OUR CHILDREN (toddlers at the time) at church. Yes we did. Feel free to roll your eyes and shake your head. We deserve it.

Jim had an elder's meeting and I had a ladies' prayer gathering before our evening service. We had taken two cars to church because Jim's meeting was scheduled several hours ahead of mine and I didn't want the kids in the nursery for an extended period. So much for noble motherhood. I came later with the kids, dropped them off at the nursery, and headed to my prayer meeting. But I grew ill during the meeting and had to go home. I asked a friend to let Jim know. (This was 1997, and the Clarks hadn't bought into the latest trend—a personal cell phone for each spouse.)

Much to my horror, Jim came through the door alone when he arrived home. My blood pressure dropped to the floor. "Where are *my* children?!"

"You brought them to church," he said. "It is logical to assume you'd bring them home."

I tried to ignore the nausea that fought for my attention as I walked toward the phone. "When you get a message that your wife is ill, it is *logical* to assume she may need you to pick up the kids!"

Before I could reach the phone, our children's coordinator, Kathy Jones, knocked on the door, opened it, and walked in with my kids in tow. "You know, if you go home, I'll find you!" She laughed and told me she heard everything about me being sick and assumed there had been a miscommunication.

The kids were all smiles and sporting treats from McDonald's. Nathan, who was three then, said, "She bought us fries, Mom, to help with the trauma." He didn't even know what the word "trauma" meant.

I burst into tears, but to this day, my daughter sees this as a happy memory. "I mean, we had a swarm of moms and Miss Kathy all around us the whole time. We weren't worried about a thing," she said.

My kids could tell countless stories of family life of growing up in the church. Sometimes it was another family that needed rescue. And like that Sunday night, sometimes it was us. Through happy times and sad, the church has cheered, wept, prayed, taught, encouraged, warned, rebuked, and defended my family.

That's why it grieves me that many in their twenties and thirties say they don't believe they need the church in order to follow Jesus. In a 2019 Pew Research Center telephone survey, "only about one-in-three millennials stated they attend religious services at least once or twice a month."[1] The reasons why are diverse and hotly debated. Regardless, many parents have at least one adult child

---

1   "In U.S., Decline of Christianity Continues at Rapid Pace," Pew Research Center, October 17, 2019, https://www.pewresearch.org/.

opting out of church. And once their children grow into adults, adults have little control over children's decisions.

But we can control ours. We can evaluate our relationship with Christ and his church. If we have not taken the church seriously or been fully committed to it, we can repent and change course. We can talk openly about those changes, which may speak volumes to our adult children. So what do we parents make of the church?

Many of us have a love-hate relationship with the church and need to remember Christ loved the church and gave himself for her. In Ephesians, Paul describes the church as the bride of Christ (Eph. 5:25–27). Marriage can be challenging, but it is worth it, especially this one, as the church is the primary vehicle God uses to communicate a picture of redemption. She also happens to be one of the greatest allies for Christian parents of adult children.

When the Church Talks to Your Adult Child

Remember how Misty Smith pursued reconciliation with her adult daughters after drug rehab? At first, her younger daughter was willing to meet, but Brittiany Lawton, Misty's oldest adult daughter, had been here before. She initially turned her mom down. She had survived the chaos her parents created, living with various relatives for years. The way Brittiany saw it, her mom had chosen drugs over her daughters. Yet in her quest to reconcile with Brittiany, Misty had a strong ally she was completely unaware of: the church.

Brittiany had come to Christ in her late teens and now was putting herself through school, paying her own bills, and making her own way. Still, Brittiany's church encouraged her to reconsider her response to her mom. They pledged to walk beside her if she took a risk to walk the road toward reconciliation.

Brittiany wanted a new life, free from the pain of the past. "But you can't get a new mom," she said. "Even if I had a choice for a new mom, I wanted that relationship with my real mom. I may have said I didn't, but deep down inside, that wasn't honest. She's my mom."

Over the next year, Brittiany would meet with her mom's counselor, and Brittiany's discipleship group listened to and prayed for her. When the big day came for her to meet with her mom, her discipleship group was on mission to pray. That year was filled with two steps forward, sometimes one step back, and moments that made steady progress toward where Misty and Brittiany are today: reconciled. "I am proud of my mom and what she's overcome," Brittiany said. "We still have some work to do, but we are talking and listening. I can say I really enjoy being with her."

Overall, the love and support of her sisters in Christ helped Brittiany find the courage to risk reconciliation. They also reminded her of the greater reconciliation that Christ made possible through his shed blood.

When the Church Won't Talk to Your Adult Child

On the other hand, the church, through her very human pastors and teachers, can sometimes disappoint a parent who seeks help for their adult child. Monica's son had fallen into heretical teaching and sexual sin. She prayed to God and begged her bishop to speak with her son. But the bishop turned her down because he didn't believe her son was open to hearing from him. Instead, he instructed her to "leave him alone for a time, only pray to God for him; he will of himself, by reading, discover what that error is, and how great its impiety."[2]

The bishop's response didn't sit well with Monica. She had already been wearing out the floor with her pacing and prayers. Like so many parents, she found the church's response to her family crisis disappointing. But she didn't hold a grudge and plan to change churches. No; instead, this desperate woman drove the bishop slap crazy. Her son later wrote that the bishop, "vexed at her importunity, exclaimed, 'Go thy way, and God bless thee, for it is impossible that the son of these tears should perish.' "[3]

This blanket assurance might not have been wise for the bishop to offer her at the time, but his words nonetheless spurred Monica on to continue to pray. In fact, she drenched the ground with her prayers and tears—for nine years. Her son, you may have guessed by now, was Augustine. Augustine's conversion took longer than Monica dared dream, but she stayed the course and continued to pray, fueled by the bishop's encouragement.

When Shame Comes to Church

When we come to church, we hear that we've all "sinned and fall short of the glory of God" (Rom. 3:23). We learn that Jesus died to pay our debt (Rom. 3:23–25). We also discover grace that is greater than all our sin. We discover, in Christ, that God sees us as clothed in Jesus's righteousness (2 Cor. 5:21; Isa. 61:10). As

---

2   Augustine, *The Confessions of St. Augustine*, trans. J. G. Pilkington (Garden City, NY: International Collectors Library American Headquarters), 59.

3   Augustine, *Confessions*, 59.

we mature in faith, we rest in the confidence that God loves us unconditionally, and we can feel secure in his love. But we don't always experience that same grace and love with our brothers and sisters in Christ. Instead, we may experience the contagious disease of self-righteousness.

In 2015, a British newspaper published an anonymous letter from a mother to her estranged son. She wrote:

> I avoid any conversation about you; I can't stand questions about how you are doing. I deflect them and reverse them until I come across as being cold and closed up. I won't be pitied, especially by those who will make judgments or will inevitably pat themselves on the back for their own parental success, in comparison with my shabby rejection. Yes, I have become paranoid—I resent what seems to be everyone else having children who enjoy their company, who have meals with them, and talk things through with them.[4]

From the need to post anonymously to the crusty tone, you can feel the underlying sense of shame that pervades this woman's heart. She can't shake it, even as she declares publicly who she resents and how she plans to deflect their questions, pity, and comparisons. Could she have a different experience at church?

Perhaps you've observed or lived the following scenario. While sipping coffee before Sunday school, a parent shares with several of her peers about a delightful visit with her

4   "A Letter to . . . My Estranged Son—Please Come Back to Me," *Guardian,* September 19, 2015, https://www.theguardian.com/.

adult daughter and grandchild. She whips out the proverbial bragging-rights pictures. Another mother of an estranged adult son wonders, Can I share that I have not spoken to my son in eight months?

When she finally has the courage to talk about her circumstance and ask for prayer, the group grows awkwardly quiet. Satan uses this situation to infect this mom with an enemy to her soul: isolating shame. He convinces her she is alone and that the rift in her family is due to her failing as a parent.

However, the faithful preaching of God's word and a right response to it can defend a parent against this kind of spiritual assault. Pastor Kevin Smith of New City Fellowship preached through a series on the Gospel of John. When he came to chapter 7, he highlighted the family drama that played out in the scene. In this passage, Jesus was interacting with his brothers, who appeared to be giving Jesus ministry advice. Pastor Smith read verses 3–5: "Leave here and go to Judea, that your disciples also may see the works you are doing. For no one works in secret if he seeks to be known openly. If you do these things, show yourself to the world. For not even his brothers believed in him."

Pastor Smith said,

His own family isn't with him. I think this could have been one of the loneliest moments for our Lord Jesus—when your family doesn't believe in you, it cuts you to the heart. Our Lord Jesus—are you watching this? He had family drama. Can I offer something? A little bit of encouragement to parents just for a minute? The Enemy wants to just crush you about your children's decisions.[5]

Imagine if our hurting mom were sitting in that pew. At least one parent grieving over an adult child was sitting there. Pastor Smith continued,

> Are you greater than Jesus? They had the ultimate One right there in the family. They watched him grow up. They watched him become a man. We think he was about thirty years old here. They watched him take his place in synagogue—watched him take up the Torah, the Word of God. They watched him all their lives, and yet their hearts were hard.[6]

Murmurs of "Amen" and "Right, right" bubbled up throughout the congregation. The church, led by their pastor, checked shame and isolation at the door.

If you're a hurting parent, you long for the body of Christ to greet your family with compassion, without the assumption that your problems stem from parental mistakes. If you've never received that assurance, let's establish it here. Certainly, parental dysfunction and sinful behavior cause some adult-parent estrangements, but not all. There is no guarantee that godly parenting will lead to a healthy adult-child relationship. This also means that parents without challenges cannot assume that they are without sin in their parenting.

5   Kevin Smith, "The Jesus We Need to Know: Timing Is Everything," New City Fellowship, September 25, 2022, 57:46, https://www.youtube.com/.
6   Smith, "The Jesus We Need to Know," 57:46.

You've probably heard this passage many times: "Train up a child in the way he should go; even when he is old he will not depart from it" (Prov. 22:6). However, like much of the wisdom in this biblical book, this is a generally true statement about human behavior, not a universal truth. We have examples of saints in the Bible whose children misbehaved, from pastor's children (e.g., Eli's boys) to the sons of good kings (e.g., David). The ultimate parent, the Lord, also lamented over his wayward children: "Hear, O heavens, and give ear, O earth; for the LORD has spoken: 'Children have I reared and brought up, but they have rebelled against me'" (Isa. 1:2).

The Benefits of the Church

Sometimes parents of estranged adult children feel shame when no one has condemned them. This can be true when a parent shares this hurt and church members are caught off guard—they truly don't know how to help or even what to say. Other times, overzealous church leaders communicate shame to parents when they misunderstand the circumstances. Church members of younger children may look for flaws in estranged parents out of fear—to reassure themselves that their own children will not follow a similar path.

Overall, parents need to give themselves grace as well as extend grace to others when their relationship with their adult children causes them pain and attending church is difficult. But despite the struggles, there is help for parents through the local church. Here are some ways to find it:

Find a kindred spirit. Parents who have previously endured estrangement with their adult children are in a unique position to offer empathy to other parents who are struggling with the same situation. They can be prayer partners and listening ears in many tough circumstances. This can dispel the myth that parents are alone in their struggles.

"Weep with those who weep" (Rom. 12:15). Job's friends did a good job of consoling him—until they opened their mouths. Similarly, often the first, best care for a hurting parent is a sense of presence and empathy in their pain. In fact, even parents who need confrontation and accountability can receive those best when the church first loves them and listens to their concerns. Don't be shy about letting friends in your church know when you are not doing well and you need empathy and support more than advice.

Call for the elders. I've heard many church members lament that their elder or deacon never called them during a crisis. But the Bible gives a specific exhortation for laity to take the initiative in requesting visitation from church leadership (James 5:13–14). Leaders cannot read minds. How do we expect them to help if we don't tell them about our need? We don't have to be physically sick to call them. Our need can be a sickness of heart or soul.

Join a small group. Bible studies, small groups, and Sunday school classes can shrink the off-putting size of a large church into a smaller, more intimate community. They also create an opportunity for parents to study and pray together. In our small groups through the years, I've had friends who have buried children, and we've wept together at the grave. We've also seen miraculous recoveries and rejoiced when they occurred. We've helped each other move. Their kids feel like ours. When a friend's son hit a rough patch with his dad, the son called my husband. "Can you meet my dad for breakfast? You know, see how things are going at home and all?" Behind this boy's call was an SOS of sorts. My husband called his dad right after talking with his son, never letting on the young man prompted him to do it.

Accept instruction and redirection. This book is peppered with instances of my parental failure, often discovered by church members who loved me enough to confront me. (After all, no one wants to read a book titled *How I Was a Superstar at Parenting.*) These stories show how the church is a safe place to build relationships with people who can speak into your life with both truth and love in a way that refreshes your soul. I am grateful for the many men and women who loved my husband and me enough to tell us when we were wrong at the right time and in the right way. My children are especially grateful.

If you feel that church is irrelevant, how will you build lifelong relationships that are safe, faithful, and loving enough to redirect you when you miss the mark with your kids? And if you aren't in church, who are your kids going to feel comfortable enough in calling when they don't feel they can come directly to you? It is all too easy to slip into the false mindset of deterministic parenting that believes right behavior will always lead to good outcomes and wrong behavior will always lead to bad outcomes. No; we are saved by grace alone, through faith alone. I thank God for wiser parents in the church who offered my husband and me instruction and encouragement in raising our children.

Overall, this mutual exhortation builds up the body of Christ unto the next generation. Our children learn that the church is a resource for them as well as their parents. They learn that God requires obedience and submission from all believers, not just women and children.

Pay attention to God's word preached and taught. "All Scripture is breathed out by God and profitable for teaching, for reproof, for correction, and for training in righteousness, that the man of God may be complete, equipped for every good work" (2 Tim. 3:16–17). God's word is our best tool to equip us for parenting. He uses it to bring instruction, conviction, and repentance. And when our adult children see true change in us as parents, they are more likely to hear the words we speak to them. Yet, it isn't enough to read the Bible on your own at home. You also need to hear God's word preached in the presence of your brothers and sisters in Christ.

Make Public Worship a Habit

All of these benefits are uniquely found in the church, so it is important to make it a priority in your life. Of course, there may be circumstances beyond your control that keep you away for a season. My job as a cardiac nurse kept me away from worship for many Sundays of my career. But as far as it depends on you, make public worship a priority.

I have often heard stories of people who suffered harm at a church and now opt to stay home. They've tried to work through leadership channels to resolve their situation but received little or no response. It's understandable they would find returning even to a different church challenging. God shares anger and grief at wrong done to one of his own and he will repay (Rom. 12:19). If you need to change churches, then do so. If you need to go to counseling to process what happened, then do it. But whatever you do, do not let the unwise or evil behavior of someone deprive you of the means of grace God uses for your spiritual growth.

Unfortunately, this is what someone does when they opt out of church because they struggle to get along with certain members. If this is you, imagine yourself explaining your reasons for opting out of church to your brothers and sisters half a world away who attend worship at risk of their lives or the lives of their family. How might that sound to them? Remember, even as adults, your children also watch how you live.

You might be tempted to watch the service online instead of attending in person, but in doing so you would miss gathering together with your brothers and sisters in Christ. You would never know what your "Amen" might do to encourage another struggling soul. You'll never know what your voice in song might do to encourage an aching heart.

I find great relief in knowing that when Scripture commands us to sing to the Lord, it exhorts us to make a joyful noise. What comes out of my mouth each Sunday is more of a noise than a song, but one Sunday, my voice sounded much better. I ought to give the music director a call, I thought. Bet he could use another alto. Reality set in when I saw the Long family behind me. The Longs, with their ten children, could rival the von Trapp Family singers. No wonder my voice improved! That is how the church works—better together.

Weeks after my husband Jim died, I couldn't find the strength to sing at all. I could barely make my way to church and sit in the pew. But the Long family could sing. And the Johnsons. The Marrineauxs. The Beadreaus. The Hubbards.

Brokenhearted over your adult child? Feeling too unworthy for church? Jesus died for the unworthy. Come to church and let the people of Christ sing to you, for you, and over you until you have strength to sing again. Your very soul needs this. Colossians 3:16 exhorts us, "Let the word of Christ dwell in you richly, teaching and admonishing one another in all wisdom, singing psalms and hymns and spiritual songs, with thankfulness in your hearts to God."

Discussion Questions

1. Can you share a time when you reached out for help from the church and were disappointed with the response?

2. Sometimes we look to the church to help correct our adult children. How often do we honestly look to the church to correct ourselves? Why or why not?

3. Have you ever felt as if you didn't want to go to church because of a family situation at home? What would make it easier to choose to go?

4. Sometimes hurting parents need a sense of presence before they hear words of advice. How can we know what to speak and when?

5. Are you part of a small group of any kind in your church? If so, in what ways has that group strengthened your faith and supported you as a parent?

6. Do you know who the elders and deacons in your church are? What do you need from your church leaders? How can you communicate that to them?

7. Read Ephesians 2:1–3. These verses describe who we were apart from God. How do they inform our sense of unworthiness and shame when coming to church?

8. Read Ephesians 2:4–9. How do these verses help us understand our standing before God in Christ? How do they inform our understanding of our relationship to one another? What is this passage saying to the parent who feels too ashamed to come to church?

6

Patience

FOR EVERY HEARTACHE, there's a country song. Martina Mc-
Bride, mother of three daughters, was traveling on the road with
the Warren Brothers when they started talking about family,
passing time, and teenagers. Martina shared how fast parents can
go from being the center of a child's universe to watching them
become more focused on their friends and gaining independence.
Out of that conversation came the slightly irreverent hit *Teenage
Daughters*, written by the trio, which speaks of teenage rebellion
and kids who "think they know everything."[1] "I'm not surprised
when people tell me how much they relate to this song," said
McBride, "even the dads who were 'Prince Charming' in their
little girl's world until she discovered boys."[2]

The teen years started a battle for many parents who still feel
as if they are at war. You think, "My kid should be over this by

---

1   Jeffrey B. Remz, "Martina McBride Sings of Teenage Daughters," *Country Standard
    Time*, March 15, 2011, https://www.countrystandardtime.com/.
2   Remz, "Martina McBride Sings of Teenage Daughters."

now" regarding an addiction, a bad relationship, or a rejection of your values. You've prayed and begged God to do something about it for years. Shouldn't your adult child be in a better place? Yet God doesn't heal him, convict him, or even seem to grant you peace. You recognize that the people God places in our lives aren't accidents. They are his assignment. Yet, you still feel overwhelmed and without answers. Do you have the courage to pray for patience when you hit this point?

Apart from Christ, we are only worthy of condemnation, and the only thing we have earned before God is his wrath. But in Christ, he makes all things new. In Christ, we have access to the Holy Spirit, through whom we can be patient, humble, kind, faithful, and self-controlled.

In the second half of this book, we're going to examine the fruit of the Spirit and learn how they might serve us in our relationships with our adult children. We begin with patience. Patience might not receive the high press that love, joy, and peace do, but patience is a key ingredient in healthy relationships, especially with our children.

Patience

We can define patience as the ability to bear up when faced with trouble or provocation. A patient person endures much for a long time before becoming angry. Picture an oversized pot of water on the stove, waiting to come to a full boil, and a cook waiting for the water to bubble and steam to rise. Patient people are like that. They don't haul off and smack someone, and they also don't gripe or inwardly brood.

Scripture illustrates two kinds of patience. The first is patience in circumstances and the second is patience with people. The second is often the tougher assignment. Let's look at James 5, a passage that unpacks patience: "Be patient, therefore, brothers, until the coming of the Lord. See how the farmer waits for the precious fruit of the earth, being patient about it, until it receives the early and the late rains. You also, be patient. Establish your hearts, for the coming of the Lord is at hand" (5:7–8).

In the Palestinian climate, although most of the rains fell between December and February, fall and spring rains became critical to a good harvest. If a farmer grew antsy and harvested too soon, the crop would not yield nearly the volume it would have had he patiently waited. Waiting was the hard part. He could easily have jumped ahead and harvested his crop, fearing the rains would come too little, too late, or not at all.[3]

As parents of adult children, maybe of ones we'd call "late bloomers," we can relate. An impulsive adult son might not take his dad's advice about delaying gratification in order to save his money, and it might become excruciating for a penny-pinching father to watch. He fervently prays for his son to be more careful with his limited funds. All the while, God is also planning to build patience in Dad. As his son's checkbook goes from black to red, patience may mean Dad must step back from the temptation to rescue him and instead allow God to work his plan. Then, when the son experiences the consequences of his choices, Dad wraps his arms around him and says, "I love you, and I'll be with you" instead of "I told you so." This weak, vulnerable, praying dad reflects the character of God, who is "merciful and gracious, slow to anger and abounding in steadfast love" (Ps. 103:8).

---

3   Grant R. Osborne, study notes to James in the *ESV Study Bible* (Wheaton, IL: Crossway, 2016), 2632.

The Opposite of Patience

Let's look at the next verses in James 5:

> Do not grumble against one another, brothers, so that you may
> not be judged; behold, the Judge is standing at the door. As an
> example of suffering and patience, brothers, take the prophets
> who spoke in the name of the Lord. Behold, we consider those
> blessed who remained steadfast. You have heard of the steadfast-
> ness of Job, and you have seen the purpose of the Lord, how
> the Lord is compassionate and merciful. (5:9–11)

Grumbling, which is a form of impatience, will invoke the
judgment of God. It feeds resentment, bitterness, and anger.
Although we might delude ourselves into thinking our ranting is
against a person, ultimately, it is against the Lord.

Seeing Job's name mentioned in this passage convicts me. If
ever there was a person who battled the temptation to grumble,
it would be Job. He was bereft of his health, children, and wealth,
and his friends proved to be pitiful comforters. His wife also offered bleak solace when she told him, "Curse God and die!" (Job
2:9). Yet, God's word says that "in all this Job did not sin or charge
God with wrong" (Job 1:22).

Signs of Grumbling

While we want to avoid grumbling, it's perfectly okay to grieve
and lament before God when something breaks our hearts. How
can we know the difference? An example from Exodus might
prove helpful.

Two months after the children of Israel left Egypt as God's free nation, they encountered the Egyptian army. God miraculously delivered them by allowing them to cross the Jordan and then drowning the Egyptian army in that same river before their eyes. Yet, three days later, they grumbled about their situation.

The apostle Paul notes their behavior in 1 Corinthians 10:11, saying, "Now these things happened to them as an example, but they were written down for our instruction." Consider what "these things" include:

> The whole congregation . . . grumbled against Moses and Aaron
> . . . "Would that we had died by the hand of the LORD in the land of Egypt, when we sat by the meat pots and ate bread to the full, for you have brought us out into this wilderness to kill this whole assembly with hunger." (Ex. 16:2–3)

This passage shows us several signs of grumbling. Let's look more closely at a few now.

An absence of prayer. God delivered the Israelites from slavery and a massive Egyptian army. Did it not occur to them that the same God could manage a hunger problem? Had they even asked him to? In a crisis, our frazzled emotions can easily jump into the driver's seat and take over. Impatience often acts before seeking God's face for direction. Patience accesses the part of one's brain (the frontal lobe) that knows the Lord's faithfulness and cries out to him.

Romanticizing the past. "Sat by the meat pots of meat and ate bread to the full" does not accurately describe the Israelites' situation as slaves in Egypt. No—"the people of Israel groaned because of their slavery and cried out for help" (Ex. 2:23). If the present isn't to your liking, it's very easy to look back and think the past was much better than it was when you are feeling impatient.

Exaggerating and lying. The grumbling Israelites complained to God, "You have brought us out into this wilderness to kill this whole assembly with hunger." When we encounter stress, pain, or suffering, we'll say things that we don't mean or are false. So when we suffer, we need to focus on what is objectively true about God and our circumstances.

Self-pity and whining. While bitterness is a response to a circumstance that pushes anger further inward, self-pity typically begins on the inside and then spreads to others. Self-pity is contagious and sets one up for more dangerous sins. Typically, grumbling is vocal, but it can also be more subtle. We can take our complaints inward, moping around as we do errands, with only an occasional sigh to give us away. Our adult children can spot this, though we might congratulate ourselves on the stiff upper lip we've managed to maintain. We know our hearts aren't right. But even unbelievers know how to be outwardly moral. Christians ought to consider the inward state of their hearts.

The Heart of Impatience

Impatience might seem obvious. We've all experienced the impatient driver behind us in a construction zone on the freeway. Perhaps you've heard someone sigh behind you when you waited at the DMV with your sixteen-year-old. Impatient people can scorn others, put them down, offer cutting humor, and engage in gossip. They can also be downright cold. But less obviously, impatience can become inward, unspoken resentment and bitterness. This can then devolve into an even more extreme response: revenge.

While we may believe it's a person who causes our angst, our real beef is with God. The health of our horizontal relationships with others always comes back to the health of the vertical relationship we have with God. Even though, in our moments of frustration, we're not really asking God to stop being the Lord of all the universe, we do wonder if he could just let us control our corner.

But our God is not easily tamed. He won't respond like a pet or answer a wish list as if he were Santa Claus. And this is good news. It means that our lives with a sovereign God aren't on a plan B. He already factored in all my sinful tendencies and foolish choices when he mapped out his will for my life. He is a good God, and we can trust him even when we can't see how things will work out.

The Patience of God

If patience is a fruit of the Spirit and not something we can muster up merely by our own efforts, then how can we foster an environment where patience can grow in our hearts? One way is to regularly ponder how God has been patient with you. Following are a few examples.

Christ never gave up on God's plan for him—to save sinners. Jesus came to earth for the sole purpose of saving your never-dying soul. And he didn't change his mind about his love for you because of your behavior. There is no game-changer or game-over moment for him. As he said in the Gospel of John, "The Father loves me, because I lay down my life that I may take it up again. No one takes it from me, but I lay it down of my own accord" (10:17–18).

Christ endured the wrath of a holy God. He experienced desertion by his closest friends, betrayal, mocking, and unspeakable physical suffering. Hebrews says that "for the joy that was set before him [he] endured the cross" (12:2). How did he do that? Patience. Praise God he didn't say, "I've had enough. You've brought this on yourself. You reap what you've sown." By his grace, our patience with our adult children can look like this too.

Christ loved us before we showed signs of repentance. Meditate on Luke 15, the parable of the prodigal son. Commenting on this parable, Russell Moore says,

> When dealing with those wandering away from the faith, we must recognize that sometimes they'll not start evaluating the deep questions of their lives until they find themselves in a situation where they don't know what to do. We must be the sort of parents and grandparents and churches who have kept open every possible connection, so that our prodigals will know how to get back home, and know we'll meet them at the road, already planning a homecoming party. . . . In many cases, the real tragedy in a family with rebellious children isn't that their parents hurt for them, but that their parents are embarrassed of them.[4]

Moore is right. Often, we parents hold a deep grudge when our children have wronged us. Yet, this is not how God loves us.

Remember Luke 15:20, where it says of the prodigal son's father, "But while he was still a long way off, his father saw him and felt compassion, and ran and embraced him and kissed him." He

4   Russell Moore, "Love Your Prodigal as Yourself," *The Gospel Coalition* (blog), September 18, 2018, https://www.thegospelcoalition.org/.

had been looking for his son, and he didn't wait to see what his son had to say. Rather, he ran to him, which was quite undignified for a man in his culture to do. There could be no doubt in the son's mind that his father loved him.

Patience is often hard to see, but this is a picture of God's loving patience with us. Kenneth E. Bailey explains,

> The father's suffering at the beginning of their estrangement has no effect on the son. He is not even aware of it. A demonstration of the father's suffering for him must be witnessed by the son. Without this, the son in his callousness will never discover the suffering of his father and will never understand that he is the cause. . . . Without the visible demonstration of costly love there can be no reconciliation.[5]

Patience at Home

As parents, our patience can be tested when our adult children refuse to heed our advice and insist on going their own way. Depending on the mistake, we might suffer embarrassment as a consequence of their poor decision. Still, this potentially frustrating circumstance might be an opportunity to reflect the character of God to your adult children.

At the funeral for her famous father, Billy Graham, Ruth Graham shared personal stories from her family history. Devastated when her marriage of twenty-one years ended in a divorce, Ruth went looking for love in all the wrong places. And she found it, just months after her divorce.

5 Kenneth E. Bailey, *The Cross and The Prodigal: Luke 15 Through the Eyes of Middle Eastern Peasants*, 2nd ed. (Downers Grove, IL: InterVarsity, 2005), 69.

"I would have told you Jesus alone was my security, but that was not the truth," Ruth said.[6] Though her parents cautioned her to wait, she married a man on New Year's Eve. What did they know about life as a single mother?

Within twenty-four hours she realized she had made a mistake. She ended up fleeing that man five weeks later. A grown woman covered with shame, Ruth's mind was filled with questions. "What was I going to say to Daddy? To my mother? I'd been such a failure. What would they say to me? 'We told you not to do it. You embarrassed us.' You don't want to embarrass your father. You really don't want to embarrass Billy Graham."[7] How could Ruth ever come home again and face her parents?

We congratulate ourselves when our children grow up to know the Lord, and they move out of our home to establish their own families. We are done. We can almost sense the smile from heaven. Whew! But are we done? For twenty-one years Billy Graham's daughter had the outward appearance of being a stable, well-adjusted woman with a godly family. But for those of us who have walked with the Lord a while, we know stability can be a facade. Live long enough and you will either be suffering the consequences of your sin or of someone you love. You will need patience to forbear and endure the trials of your adult children.

The way home for Ruth was a two-hour drive. As she emerged from the car, her dad, the beloved father whom she feared she had embarrassed, was waiting in the driveway. He wrapped his arms around her and said, "Welcome home."

6   Ruth Graham, "Forgiving My Father," Life Today, November 13, 2019, 1:40, https://www.youtube.com/.

7   Graham, "Forgiving My Father," 1:40.

"There was no shame, no blame, no condemnation that day," Ruth said. "Just unconditional love. My father was not God, but he showed me what God was like. When we come to God with our sin, our brokenness, our failure, God says, 'Welcome home.'"[8]

Reinforcing Patience

Clearly, patience is a Christian virtue. But, as we've seen, it can be hard to identify and even harder to exhibit. Let's look at some practical things we can do to reinforce patience, thus making it easier to exhibit when we're tempted to grumble.

Practice being courteous. I am embarrassed to see Christians who have a poor testimony at restaurants, grocery stores, or on the phone with customer service. Behind the phone call, counter, or cash register is an image bearer of God. Remember that before you speak.

Be open to feedback about your behavior. This is especially important with your adult children. What you might perceive as perfectly fine may seem to them as rude. Case in point was the cell phone debacle I mentioned in chapter 2. When I had my phone in front of me, checking messages while chatting with my daughter, I thought I was multitasking. My daughter saw a mother only half listening to her. In addition to being open to your children's feedback, make sure you have other adults in your life who are willing to speak with you honestly about your relationship with your adult children.

Free up your schedule. This might be hard to hear, but if a jam-packed schedule is making you impatient, rude, inwardly resentful, and bitter, then you are too busy.

8 Ruth Graham, "Service for Billy Graham," Washington Post, March 2, 2018, 1:33, https://www.youtube.com/.

Remember that you need patience from others. Seriously. You get on other people's nerves. My big brother, Mike, had the patience of Job when he taught me to drive a manual transmission. He was motivated by mercy. He had endured a poor instructor and a humiliating experience when he was learning to drive a manual car and was determined to deliver me from the same fate. The lesson wasn't a fun time for him, yet he never once raised his voice or let go a sigh. In fact, he smiled and reassured me. "Don't worry sis. It's Dad's car, not mine." I gave him a fist bump and tried again. I was keenly aware in that situation that I could tax my brother's patience. This memory has made me wonder if there are other circumstances where I am unaware of how exasperating my behavior can be to others.

Don't think too highly of yourself. The apostle Paul said, "If I should wish to boast, I would not be a fool, for I would be speaking the truth; but I refrain from it, so that no one may think more of me than he sees in me or hears from me" (2 Cor. 12:6). If he had this concern, so should we. Think of someone you know who you might describe as having an ego problem. Are they a joy to be around? When we think too highly of ourselves, we tax the patience of those around us.

Get a grip on your anger. The Bible says, "Be angry and do not sin; do not let the sun go down on your anger, and give no opportunity to the devil" (Eph. 4:26–27). This passage shows us that anger isn't inherently sinful. Righteous anger defends good or tries to restrain evil. Thus, if our adult child makes sinful choices that place her in harm's way (like living with an abusive boyfriend), we parents get rightfully angry. But it's tricky to separate the sin from the sinner; our motives are rarely wholly pure. So if we are angry for righteous reasons, we would do well to have others walking beside us, helping us stay focused on attacking the problem and not the people involved. We see a bad boyfriend as the enemy, but we fight a greater foe. We do not wrestle with "flesh and blood" (Eph. 6:12). Directing our fight to the real enemy will help us avoid the kind of sinful anger that thwarts patience.

Guard your speech. We all say things we might later regret. Ephesians 4:29 and 31 commands, "Let no corrupting talk come out of your mouths, but only such as is good for building up, as fits the occasion, that it may give grace to those who hear. . . . Let all bitterness and wrath and anger and clamor and slander be put away from you, along with all malice." To me, "corrupting talk" means putrid talk—decaying, angered, clamorous, slanderous talk. It is the kind of talk the Israelites engaged in after the exodus. When we are defending our pride, our parental authority, or a precious idol, this kind of anger can rear its ugly head. To reinforce patience, we have to watch what we say, especially when feeling sensitive.

Be kind and forgive. Ephesians exhorts us to "be kind to one another, tenderhearted, forgiving one another, as God in Christ forgave you" (4:32). We will address kindness in the next chapter but, suffice it to say, forgiveness often requires us to practice patience.

Watch out for growing bitterness. Hebrews says, "See to it that no one fails to obtain the grace of God; that no 'root of bitterness' springs up and causes trouble, and by it many become defiled" (12:15). Some roots grow downward and can be hard to see. It may be difficult to pull them up if they're allowed to flourish too long, so we must keep an eye out and get rid of them immediately. We cannot be both patient and bitter people.

Flee to the Savior. We cannot live a righteous life apart from Christ. We need him, as the hymn says, "every hour," all the more so when it comes to trials with our children.[9] Our adult children will try our patience, precisely because we have higher expectations of them. The amusing thing is they may say the same thing about us to their friends. As you pray for your sons and daughters, consider this: As their parent, God has called you to be an instrument of sanctification in their life. But could it be God has called your adult child, with all his struggles and difficulties, to that same duty in your life as well? God may use him to produce "steadfastness . . . that you may be perfect and complete, lacking in nothing" (James 1:2–4).

When my kids were young adults, I was a stressed-out, overloaded mom who had three calendars full of responsibilities that kept me irritable and absent from them when they desperately needed my attention. I was too busy to be patient. I began asking the Lord to give me tangible opportunities to show my kids they were a priority in my life. In the Lord's mercy, I overheard Anna tell a friend that her "lifelong dream was to attend a Martina McBride concert." Among the lifelong dreams on her list, that was doable. I canceled a few things on the to-do list and moved other things off my list entirely. It was more than worth it when I put the tickets in Anna's hand and said, "Pack your bags."

Anna's jaw dropped and she stared at the tickets in disbelief. I grinned. "We're headed to Nashville. Reckon your buddy Katie

9   Robert Lowry and Annie S. Hawkes, "I Need Thee Every Hour" (1872).

would want to come too? I bought an extra ticket just in case." I still remember the squeal that came out of her mouth and the hug that followed.

On a balmy July night in Nashville, Anna and I held our cell phones high and watched them glow in the dark with about fifty thousand others while we listened Martina sing "In My Daughter's Eyes," a much a softer, sentimental tune than "Teenage Daughters." And we made some memories.

Discussion Questions

1. Do you find it more difficult to exhibit patience regarding circumstances or people?

2. It is not a sin to lament before the Lord, but it is to grumble. How do we know when we've left the arena of lament and stumbled into grumbling?

3. What are some signs of grumbling that we saw in Exodus that you struggle with today?

4. How has God been patient with you?

5. How can understanding God's patience with us inform our patience with our children?

6. Has your schedule made you irritable and negatively affected your relationships with your adult children? What would it take to rectify that?

7. Read Proverbs 25:15. Though this verse speaks of persuading rulers, what might we learn from it about the posture we should take when communicating with our adult child?

8. Read Romans 8:24–25. Hope is mentioned five times in these two verses. What is the hope that we wait for with patience? Earlier in the passage, Paul assures us whatever suffering we are enduring will be worth it. How does this promise enable you to bear the difficulties with your adult child with patience?

7

Goodness and Kindness

"EVERYONE LIKES TO DECORATE for Christmas, but no one wants to help me take the decorations down." Usually, this comment fell on deaf ears, but I complained every year nonetheless. "I'm helping!" Anna said. Ah, kudos to the firstborn. Now she put a pinch of pressure on my husband.

Jim sighed and said, "All right. I can help in the bonus room."

Clever, Jim Clark—there was only one small tree in there. Jim went to his task, and I gave Anna a to-do list. She finished in short order, so I gave her another list, and then another. I looked toward the bonus room; Jim should have finished a long time ago. When Anna returned a third time, we went to check on her father.

The ornaments were packed in boxes. Then we noticed the white carpet peppered with green pine needles. A string of Christmas lights lay partially off the tree, with the ones that remained appearing to cling for dear life onto what was left of the evergreen. Jim held the fir upside down between his knees, freeing both hands to grasp those stubborn lights. He looked up at us, his face reddened by exertion. "These lights," he said, pausing for breath with each syllable, "are an absolute pain to get off this stinking tree!" I took the tree from him and brushed stray pine needles off his jeans.

"Thank you, honey. We can take it from here. Sorry about all this. Seems like no good deed—"

"—goes unpunished. You got that right!" Jim nodded and headed upstairs.

As I looked at my decimated tree, I explained to a perplexed Anna that good timing is a key element of healthy communication. Yes, Dad didn't need to remove the lights at all because it was a pre-lit tree, but now wasn't the time to inform him of that little detail. These are the kinds of things a mother tells her daughter in order to save her future marriage.

Please and Thank-You

Sometimes when we engage in a good deed, it does seem as though we are punished for our kindness. Goodness and kindness seem almost naive and unwise in today's dangerous world. If you are bold enough to be kind, your actions might not be punished, but they might be unappreciated, even if the recipient is an adult child. Worse, your adult children may grow to expect the undeserved kindness as a duty owed them.

Consider a dad who stayed up all night to help his son with his college paper. The son waited until the last minute to tell him about it. Dad dropped everything to work on the emergency. His son moaned about having to get up the next day for class at seven o'clock, and Dad winced, knowing his day started at five o'clock.

The next morning, the son texted his dad: "I am so dead! Forgot my paper at the house! Can you drop it by the school? It's due before 1:30. Thnx!" Dad bowed out from work on his lunch break to retrieve it for him. "Thnx!" was all the acknowledgment he received. Should the dad say something?

On the other hand, some people can have unrealistically high expectations when it comes to expressing gratitude. I had a relative who insisted on getting a formal thank-you note whenever she sent a gift. Until it arrived in her mailbox, she was frustrated and resentful toward the gift's recipient.

The written thank-you thing was embedded in her DNA. But she made me think of my kids. Am I doing this to them in some way? I might not verbalize it, but do I resent the lack of response I might receive when I try to help? The goal of our goodness and kindness is not to be thanked. In fact, Scripture warns against expecting a reward for our good deeds (Matt. 6:1–4). As parents, it isn't wrong to expect our children to honor us—after all, they are commanded to do so by God (Ex. 20:12). But we get into trouble when we insist on that honor looking a certain way and with a certain regularity that Scripture never commands. I knew this in my head, but was I okay when I felt ignored or taken for granted? I had to remember the source of goodness and kindness in order to change.

Goodness

One of the very first lessons we learn about God is that he is loving and good. The psalmist invites us to engage our senses in order to worship this God, saying, "Oh, taste and see that the LORD is good!" (Ps. 34:8).

The Greek word for goodness is *agathōsunē*. It means "being the same person in every situation, rather than a phony or a hypocrite."[1] In other words, it means being a person of integrity, trustworthiness, and consistencey. No Dr. Jekyll and Mr. Hyde. George Bethune wrote in his commentary on the fruit of the Spirit,

> The good man is not content with giving to the poor, and relieving the wretched, and exhorting the sinner, while he is harsh to his family, and overbearing to his servants [employees], and haughty to his neighbours. . . . The grace of God can dwell in strange places, but it is difficult to conceive how a peevish, passionate man, careless of others' feelings and comforts, can be a good man, though he may have built a hospital and fed a city with bread.[2]

You might know a person who is "careless with the feelings of others" and yet has accomplished much for their community, led a corporation, or chaired the women's committee at church. This isn't the Bible's definition of "good." You may need to look in the mirror and ask yourself, do I resemble this person? In contrast, our God is the same today, yesterday, and forever. We can be thankful he never changes.

Goodness Has a Purpose

In general, God's word associates good and goodness with doing something. The master in Jesus's parable said, "Well *done, good and faithful servant*" (Matt. 25:23). When creating the

---

1   Tim Keller, *Galatians For You* (Charlotte, NC: Good Book, 2013), 154.
2   George Washington Bethune, *The Fruit of the Spirit*, 3rd ed. (Philadelphia: Mentz and Rovoudt, 1845), 182.

universe, God called his handiwork good, and in giving human beings dominion over his creation, he gave them something to do—a purpose.

This purpose is clearly laid out in Ephesians 2:10: "we are his workmanship, created in Christ Jesus for good works, which God prepared beforehand, that we should walk in them." Purpose is part of what gives our lives meaning. Purpose, unlike our identity, isn't a constant. We may hold a certain job for ten years and then move on to another. Similarly, we might find ourselves working in more than one area of ministry over the course of our lives. We need to constantly ask the Lord, How are you calling me to serve in this season of my life? But our main purpose doesn't change.

When adult kids leave home, many parents grow anxious and find themselves seeking to control their kids because they aren't ready to let them go. These parents have confused their purpose with their identity. Our identity is in Christ, and in him we remain secure. We are free to take a deep breath, trust him, and let our children go.

The Opposite of Goodness

The opposite of goodness is hypocrisy. As parents, we need to strive for consistency. When we are phony, it's our family who is first to recognize this, sometimes even before we do.

Years ago, a parent asked my husband to talk with his college junior because his "grades had begun to slip." By slipping, his father meant that in one subject an A-plus dipped to a B-minus. This caused my husband to generate his famous Vulcanlike raised eyebrow. Then the dad mentioned his son was also bowing out of church on Sunday. He asked Jim to talk to him.

When Jim approached the son, the son might have thought he would receive a sermon, but he couldn't have been more wrong. He told Jim that he was taking one of the most challenging courses in chemical engineering—thermodynamics—and recently learned his dad was having an affair. It wreaked havoc in his heart, especially on Sunday, to watch his dad nod an amen at key points in the sermon or put an arm around his mom while knowing his dad wasn't the same person at home. It overwhelmed and grieved him at the same time. He didn't know what to do. No wonder he had difficulty concentrating on a challenging course. And how sad that his dad wanted the speck out of his son's eye but seemed unconcerned about the log in his own (Matt. 7:5)! I can only imagine the look of relief on that boy's face when Jim told him he was an engineer and that thermodynamics almost made him change majors. Jim prayed with him and promised to speak with his dad about his marriage.

Our hypocrisy may not be as blatant as this, but, like our spouses, our children see us in our most weakened, tired, and frustrated moments. If we aren't honest and humble about our frailty, they won't hear us when we seek to speak into their lives.

Kindness

Similar to goodness is the character quality of kindness. Goodness and kindness are often thought of as interchangeable traits, but they have distinct differences. While goodness focuses on the inward man—not being a hypocrite—kindness leans more outward. The Greek word for kindness is *chrēstotēs*, which means "a tender concern for others"—not weakness, not lack of strength, but "the genuine desire of a believer to treat others gently, just as the Lord treats him."[3] It is "is the grace which pervades the whole nature, mellowing all which would be harsh and austere."[4] Christian kindness isn't just common courtesy, although it is always a good thing to be courteous.

What makes kindness distinctly Christian is when it becomes a supernatural response to mistreatment and hurt. It certainly isn't random, nor free, as some secular outlets like to infer. To describe it that way robs kindness of its true identity. It is an all-out, countercultural response to meanness or outrage.

Kind Speech

Like the other fruits of the spirit, kindness can be expressed by our actions, words, and tone. It's one thing to absorb an offense and walk away; sometimes that is the right response. Yet, at other times, God may call us to respond to ugliness with a gentle but honest answer. The former is patience; the latter is kindness. This is God's response to us as sinners, for God is kind to the ungrateful and ungenerous (Luke 6:35). The apostle Paul writes, "Let all bitterness and wrath and anger and clamor and slander be put away from you, along with all malice. Be kind to one another, tenderhearted, forgiving one another, as God in Christ forgave you" (Eph. 4:31–32).

Are we kind to our kids? Are the words we speak to them respectful, regardless of how they treat us? Some parents are kinder to their bosses (who they might readily acknowledge as someone

---

3   John MacArthur, *The MacArthur New Testament Commentary: Galatians* (Chicago: Moody, 1987), 168.

4   Spiros Zodhiates, Warren Bakker, George Hadjiantoniou, eds., *The Complete Word Study Dictionary New Testament* (Chattanooga, TN: AMG, 1992), 1482.

they do not respect or like) than their own children. If they can be cordial to an unlikable or even evil boss, then surely (depending on their circumstances), they can be the same to their adult children. It isn't an affirmation of bad behavior to be kind to someone who behaves badly. Far from it. Recall that it's God's *kindness* that leads many to repentance (Rom. 2:4). It's also helpful to remember how God has been kind to us when we don't deserve it. Goodness and kindness are often the loudest unspoken rebuke to the most unsufferable of people. A watching world and our adult children can see the contrast immediately.

Kindness in Small Things

Kindness isn't merely the absence of rudeness or meanness. It means loving your enemies and blessing those who persecute you, in big ways and small. We might think this is only true of martyrs from church history who blessed their executors, but if we do, we miss the opportunities in our own lives to show kindness in meaningful yet small ways.

Let's say your two-year-old granddaughter is a typical toddler. She pitches a fit at the word "no," has a selective palate, and has been known to snatch a toy from her big sister on more than one occasion.

The good news is your granddaughter has a dad (your son) who is up for the challenge. At dinner, you watch your son calmly remove his angry, wailing child from her high chair and take her to her room. She was distraught over being told no when she began tossing her food on the floor. Your son steps back out of his daughter's room alone but speaks to her just before closing the door. "When you calm down, you can come back out. But you're not getting dessert." A heightened shriek comes from the bedroom as your son closes the door, breathes a weary sigh, and rejoins you at the table.

Your son has been kind to your granddaughter. Nobody said anything about a kind person being a wimp, pushover, or sap. But who's going to tell your son he's doing a great job as a parent if not you?

Recall how many adult-child estrangements start from a boatload of criticism. How about we turn things around? Why not try to see what our kids are doing right? Moms and dads of toddlers rarely have the cheerleaders they desperately need. That's *our* job as grandparents. Even if we don't agree with their parenting decisions, can we at least empathize with them about how their job is exhausting and hard? This response shouldn't be given in order to gain something from your adult child; it should simply be done in order to behave in a Christlike manner. In fact, if we have the right posture with our kids when we disagree with them, we may find an open door to speak of eternal things rather than just our current disagreements. Barry Corey, president of Biola University and author of *Love Kindness*, writes,

> The point of being kind with those with whom we disagree is not to be respected or befriended. This may never happen. Nor is the point of kindness to avoid either ruffling feathers or feeling awkward, which is cowardly "niceness." The point of kindness is to represent Jesus. Being kind to those with whom we disagree helps bring Christ to the center of the situation. Being kind is how Jesus acts. When we walk that way, we reflect and honor him, and it opens doors for what we say about him and the gospel.[5]

5   Barry H. Covey, *Love Kindness* (Carol Stream, IL: Tyndale House, 2016), 54.

Think about a disagreement that makes you feel like your relationship with your adult child is hopeless. What if it is the very thing God uses to bring them to a knowledge of the living God?

The Opposite of Kindness

The opposite of kindness is miserliness. Miserliness is marked by grasping at meanness and penuriousness (extreme stinginess).[6] Another sin that grows in the garden of miserliness is envy. We've been taught to think of envy as simply wanting what someone else has, but its roots grow much deeper than that—it is the state of being unable to rejoice in another's success. It's easy to see then how a miserly person would struggle to be kind and generous. What's not so obvious is how nice a miserly person can look on the outside.

In Mark 10, a rich young man ran to Jesus, knelt before him, and asked the million-dollar question, "What must I do to inherit eternal life?" (Mark 10:17). In many churches, this might have seemed like an opportune moment to grab the clipboard and sign him up for an upcoming class or ministry. But that's not what happened with Jesus. In their exchange, the wealthy young man assured Jesus that he had kept all the commandments from his youth. Then Jesus, "looking at him, loved him, and said to him, 'You lack one thing: go, sell all that you have and give to the poor, and you will have treasure in heaven; and come, follow me'" (10:21).

Jesus loved him. He didn't blow him off. He wasn't even annoyed, though he had every right to be. This man just told the God of all creation, "I got a perfect score on the morality

---

6   *Merriam-Webster's Collegiate Dictionary*, s.v. "miserly," accessed November 7, 2022, https://unabridged.merriam-webster.com/.

test." But Jesus didn't come back with a snarky, "You think you've kept all the commandments? Seriously?" Instead, he put his finger on the one thing the man needed to do. We don't read another word from the young man, but Scripture says he went away sad.

In the previous chapter of Mark, a father had begged Jesus to heal his son—*if* he could. Jesus was direct with this father, picking up on the key words of his initial request, "if you can," and told him, "All things are possible for one who believes" (9:23).

This father's response was quite different from the young man's: "I believe; help my unbelief" (9:24). He readily testified to his heart's desire to obey and, at the same time, willingly confessed his frailty. The rich young man was blind to his sin at the time he met with Jesus. Jesus wasn't all he wanted—he was hoping to add Jesus to his finely tuned lifestyle. He wasn't even prepared to say, "I can't do this unless you intervene in my heart." So he chose miserliness.

The God he left behind grieved too. Jesus listened intently to the father and the rich young man and used their own words to engage them. He was able to address their concerns and still point to himself. As parents, we ought to pray for God to equip us with the gift of listening ears. That may require us to sit and be still before speaking. It may look like asking questions to confirm we understand what our adult kids are saying and resisting the urge to speak quickly. The conversation may not end in agreement, but it may end with a willingness to continue talking.

Sometimes, kindness will require different approaches with different kids. One child may respond to a clear and gentle rebuke. Another, living under the same roof, may need their circumstances to bring them to the end of themselves. Your goodness and kindness should meet each of your kids, regardless of what approach is needed.

Timing Our Words

It was the end of a long day, and my husband and I sat with Anna to do some reading. Jim grabbed a newspaper to search for the funnies, but a post-Christmas sale ad caught his eye—one for Christmas trees.

"Pre-lit. Huh." He slammed the paper closed. "That tree in the bonus room?"

I stifled a chuckle and lowered my head. Anna bit her lower lip, beamed a smile, and nodded. Jim winced. "I . . . I guess I ruined that tree, didn't I?"

Anna turned into a diplomat of sorts. "Let's just say it's no longer a pre-lit Fraser fir; it's more of an un-lit shabby chic."

Smooth. You have done well, little grasshopper.

Discussion Questions

1. Have you ever felt like your adult children took your kindness for granted? How did you respond?

2. Do you feel wearied by the needs of your adult children? If so, where have you turned for help?

3. Have you ever been concerned that you were no longer being kind to your adult child but instead being overindulgent? How do we know the difference?

4. How have others (e.g., family or friends) shaped your understanding of kindness?

5. Can you recall a disagreement that seemed like it might seriously harm your relationship with your adult child but was actually used by God for his purposes?

6. Read Psalm 145. According to verse 4, how can we share the goodness of God with our adult children?

7. Verse 7 mentions God's "abundant goodness." We learned that to be good is to be consistent and to be kind is to have a tender concern for others. God has these in abundance. How does this help you better understand this verse?

8. According to verses 8–9, God extends his goodness and mercy to all, not just Israel. How else does the psalmist describe God's goodness here? How can we tangibly reflect that same kind of goodness to our adult children?

8

Gentleness and Self-Control

ONE SUNDAY MORNING, I picked a fight with my husband. Jim Clark thought he'd done a masterful job restraining his anger, but he had not fooled his wife or his children. Up until now, I'd been frozen during his rages, petrified a misstep would make things worse. Jim never raised his hand to any of us, but he could slam a door and send a glare in your direction that would make your entire body shake. To him, our crime was always obvious—leaving lights on in a vacant room, forgetting to update the checkbook, or responding too slowly to an instruction. But in reality, our offense never matched his outrage.

One Saturday night Jim had slammed the kitchen door. Anna ran to hide. And my son? For the first time that I was aware of, instead of retreating in fear, Nathan slammed his bedroom door in return. He was learning to be angry, just like his dad. Did Jim realize what he was modeling? Hard to tell. He stormed off to bed without speaking.

When you see your adult children engaged in sinful patterns, it may be time to consider whether they are simply modeling *your* behavior. If they are cold, angry, and resentful toward you, the reason might stem from your sinful pattern of behavior, which they endured for years as children and teens.

Although I was afraid of making things worse, I wondered about what might become unintended consequences for our family if I didn't confront Jim about his anger. So I started a difficult conversation with him the following day—Sunday morning before church. Yes, the timing was horrible.

The result meant we left in separate vehicles that morning, then stood in front of the church all smiles to greet visitors. Anybody else ever been here? Before we turned to take our place inside, we caught a glimpse of our kids sitting in the pew, behaving much more like adults than we had that morning. I looked at Jim and bit my lower lip. He smiled and reached for my hand as we walked in together. He would later tell me that the words I'd shared about his anger and the effect they were having on our kids were the most hurtful words I had ever told him, but they were also the most necessary for his soul. Yes, I picked a fight. But sometimes, to make things better, gentleness picks fights.

Gentleness

What is this gentleness of which the Bible speaks so often? An easiness of Spirit.[1] Self-forgetfulness. A willingness to consider others first. Submission to God in word and heart. A willingness to relinquish control without anger or resentment.[2] Overall,

---

1   Matthew Henry, *The Quest for Meekness and Quietness of Spirit* (Eugene, OR: Wipf and Stock, 2007), 17.
2   George Washington Bethune, *The Fruit of the Spirit*, 3rd ed. (Philadelphia: Mentz and Rovoudt, 1845), 140.

true, full-fledged gentleness (or meekness, as it is called in some translations) is impossible apart from the work of the Holy Spirit.

In his book *Gentle and Lowly*, Dane Ortlund notes that only once (in Matt. 11:28) did Jesus tell us about the very essence of who he is. Ortlund explains,

> In the one place in the Bible where the Son of God pulls back the veil and lets us peer way down into the core of who he is, we are not told that he is "austere and demanding in heart." We are not told that he is "exalted and dignified in heart." We are not even told that he is "joyful and generous in heart." Letting Jesus set the terms, his surprising claim is that he is "gentle and lowly in heart."[3]

How could a gentle and lowly man save us from our sins? There must be more to it than our preconceived notions. Jesus suffered as no person did when he went to the cross on our behalf. Yet he was brutally honest about his pain: "In the days of his flesh, Jesus offered up prayers and supplications, with loud cries and tears, to him who was able to save him from death, and he was heard because of his reverence. Although he was a son, he learned obedience through what he suffered" (Heb. 5:7–8).

Ever feel as if your cries to heaven about your adult children or home situation are not making it outside your body, let alone to God? Jesus's prayers were loud cries, not the grin-and-bear-it kind. And note this, parents: Jesus was heard. This is important to remember because a common fear is that being meek means

---

3   Dane Ortlund, *Gentle and Lowly* (Wheaton, IL: Crossway, 2020), 18.

being overlooked and unseen. That may be true as far as the world is concerned, but not God. In fact, these verses tell us that God heard Jesus's prayers *because* of his meekness, not in spite of it.

Thus, if you opt out of gentleness, you are opting out of Christ. Without meekness, there would be no Calvary. There would be no "humbled himself by becoming obedient to the point of death, even death on a cross" (Phil. 2:8). Jesus wasn't worried about people walking all over him. He saved the world by making himself lowly.

Surely if he saved the world this way, there will be times God will call us to follow a similar plan with our adult children. But like Christ, it doesn't mean we must suffer in silence. Sometimes gentleness refrains from speaking, and sometimes gentleness speaks. But even when gentleness calls you to speak, it will also guide you to know when you've said enough. And what connects the heart to actions? Self-control.

Self-Control

We all struggle with some aspect of self-control. Some parents don't know when to stop talking and start listening. Others overspend on their grandkids. Still others may struggle with overeating, drinking, or drug abuse, which affects their relationship with their adult children. Tim Keller defined self-control as "the ability to pursue the important over the urgent rather than to be always impulsive or uncontrolled."[4]

Self-control means thinking of your adult child's needs over your own. We did that instinctively when they were young

---

4   Timothy Keller, *Galatians For You* (Charlotte, NC: Good Book, 2013), 155.

children, but we shouldn't abandon the practice as they grow into adults. It just looks different. For example, when your adult son espouses things you find offensive, it may be easy to think you are speaking for God when you oppose him. But in your clear opposition toward his views, can you also boldly declare your love for him as your son? This is self-control.

I know parents whose adult child plays in a rock band at a local bar in their town. Rock music might be considered their least favorite genre. They also abstain from drinking alcohol because of its commonly associated sins. Yet twice a month on a Saturday night they make their way down to the bar where their son plays, order two sodas, and listen to his band. Dad jots down notes on some of the lyrics, hoping to start a discussion with his son later. When the band takes a bow, you can bet his folks are on their feet, clapping enthusiastically. Although they don't care for rock music per se, they work hard to find something about the music they do enjoy. Sometimes it's a line in the lyrics, other times it's a drum solo. They take interest in his passion.

This son once told his parents, "You don't have to come, I know you hate this sort of thing." But his dad replied, "I love you, and what interests you interests me. That's reason enough to give it a listen—oh, and the lead singer is awesome!" His son shook his head and smiled. "Do what you want then."

Month after month they came. Follow-up questions, conversations, and compliments proved they hadn't just faked their enjoyment. His son later told me, "Nobody loves like that. I had to start coming back to church with them. They were showing me who God really was."

Part of embracing the gospel is recognizing that you are not God and you are not in control of the lives of your adult children; God is in control. When you sit down with your adult child to listen to his concerns, do you allow him to finish his sentences? Do you ask questions to ensure you understand what your child is trying to say? Do you show him that what is important to him is important to you, even when you disagree? That does not mean you agree with, enable, or support any sinful habits. It means his differences (and even his sin!) don't threaten or unduly annoy you.

Relinquishing Control; Submitting to God

Gentleness and self-control often work together to grant us a pause to consider the circumstances that threaten to provoke us. When Nehemiah learned the nobles and officials in the community were exploiting their rank-and-file brothers and sisters, he said, "I was very angry when I heard their outcry and these words. *I took counsel with myself*, and I brought charges against the nobles and the officials" (Neh. 5:6–7). Before he rebuked these officials, he checked his heart. This is gentleness—maintaining an inward peace despite an outward provocation. Note that Nehemiah still rebuked the officials, but he did so with a calm spirit. This is self-control.

How might these two qualities help our relationships with our adult children? Romans 15:2 exhorts us to "please [our] neighbor for his good." That means we need to consider if our words bring about the good of our adult children as opposed to our own self-defense or desire to be right, lay down the law, or get something off our chest. In earlier years, this looked like not disciplining an unruly toddler in anger or caving to their cries for sweets when that was easier than saying no. Gentleness always considers the other person's well-being. In other words, it slows us down and makes us think before we act in a way we will regret or speak words we cannot take back. It's the Holy Spirit calling us to take a deep breath.

When You Must Speak

So, you've listened carefully. You've asked questions in a nonthreatening way. When it's your turn to speak, what would gentleness and self-control say to your adult children?

In 2 Chronicles 25, God sent an unnamed prophet to speak to King Amaziah. He asked the king, "Why have you sought the gods of a people who did not deliver their own people from your hand?" (25:15). In other words—King Amaziah, have you lost your mind? Gentleness, however, rewords the question with tact and infuses it with helpful information.

Perhaps you feel tempted to ask your adult children a similar question, but consider that "winning" an argument with a harshly toned, exaggerated question might translate into losing the war. Instead, follow the prophet's example by approaching your child with clarity, caution, and deftness.

First, the prophet was clear. He didn't question the king's heart or his feelings but pointed to specific outward sinful behavior. Second, he was cautious—the prophet explained the long-term consequences of the king's choices. Finally, he was deft. He made his point by asking a question without causing unnecessary humiliation or frustration.

The next verse says that when the king responded badly despite the care taken, the prophet stopped. God's unnamed prophet knew when to confront and when to walk away. A meek, self-controlled person knows when to speak and when it's time to back off. He doesn't engage in a shouting match, and he doesn't take it personally.

My mother-in-law, Carolyn, was a master at knowing when to speak and when to back off. If she had a concern about my parenting, she was careful to ask a nonthreatening question before offering any advice. For example, when I brought my newborn daughter home from the hospital, she noticed I didn't give her any water to drink, something she had been taught to do as a new mother. But instead of jumping to conclusions and then jumping on me, she asked, "What did the doctor tell you about the baby needing water in addition to breast milk?" I explained that doctors no longer encouraged that but, at the same time, it wouldn't hurt to try it once in a while. I told her, "I'm sure that by the time she's grown and parenting her babies, there will be a few more things that will have changed."

My prediction proved true. My children are doing a few things differently based on current expert advice and I'm not a bit worried about my grandkids. They will be fine.

Here is a takeaway for us as parents: even a prophet knew his job wasn't to change someone's heart. Too often, we parents lose sight of this. A parent may believe he knows his child's heart, mind, and motives. Yet Scripture is clear that the heart is deceitful. Who can understand it but God (Jer. 17:9)? We may feel we know what's best for our adult child, and we don't relish watching them walk down a road of folly and sin. We nag, warn, badger, and even try to manipulate circumstances to prevent disaster. But when we do this, where are we placing our ultimate trust? Certainly not in the God we are trying to point our adult children to. It is no wonder that adult children often estrange themselves from Christian parents, setting new boundaries to distance themselves from these controlling behaviors.

When Gentleness and Self-Control Are Forgotten

Thirty-one-year-old Sharon Kwon hadn't spoken with her parents in thirteen years. She wrote in a HuffPost article,

> Christianity brought us to America, and as the years went by, I found myself growing farther and farther apart from them and their life purpose of spreading God's word. My pastor father and submissive mother had only one condition for me to earn their love—to be a God-fearing, church-going Christian—but I just couldn't be that for them.
>
> I didn't know how to reconcile with the endless shame and the belief that I would never be good enough. I left home at 18 years old, making sure to put as much physical distance between me and them as possible.[5]

Sharon sought counseling and eventually became a therapist herself. As she listened to her patients, many of whom also struggled with similar family issues, she began to wonder, was she setting healthy boundaries with her parents or simply avoiding them as a means of coping with family stress? After giving this some thought, Sharon wrote her parents and asked if they would

---

5   Sharon Kwon, "My Parents And I Were Estranged For Years. Here's What Happened When We Finally Talked Again," HuffPost, November 16, 2022, https://www.huffpost .com/. All direct quotations in this section are from this source.

be willing to talk through their concerns in family therapy. To her surprise, they both agreed.

From Sharon's perspective, the sessions proved difficult because her father monopolized the conversation, interrupted her, and "rebutted every little thing [she] had to say." But their therapist, who was a Christian, told Sharon's parents, "The real issue is that you're not listening to her." She encouraged them to reiterate Sharon's words so that they could be certain they heard and understood what she had said.

Her dad balked at this suggestion. "Why should I say something that I don't agree with?" he asked. "Because otherwise you'll never get to hear what she's saying and how she truly feels," their therapist explained. Sharon wrote, "My dad did try to listen to me until he inevitably reached his breaking point and yelled at me through the [Zoom] screen, telling me to get over it and move on already."

While HuffPost does not have a follow-up article with her parents' perspective, Sharon's concerns aren't an isolated case. In the few studies conducted on estranged adult children, many of them mention feeling that their parents hadn't heard them, especially if their values differed from their parents' values. When Christian parents attempt to have discussions with their adult children, often it is the parent who storms off. As one young man told me, "Jesus loves me, this I know. But my dad? Only if I toe the line. I am never good enough for him." Remember what Sharon mentioned earlier? She struggled with "endless shame" and the belief she would "never be good enough."

Do your adult children feel they have to earn your love? Ask them. Don't assume the answer is no. If they say yes, it would be a wonderful opportunity to remind them that since we do not earn God's love, they should never be made to feel like they have to earn ours. This might lead to clearing up some misunderstanding about what God truly requires of us and what you, as a Christian, ultimately put your faith in—not your own good works but Christ's finished work. It might be the most redemptive conversation you have to date.

Restoring Sinners

I recognize all this talk on gentleness is maddening when some of you are dealing with out-of-control, angry adult children who are clearly in the wrong. You may wonder, what then? If your adult child is a believer, you have grounds to try to correct them. Galatians 6:1 says, "Brothers, if anyone is caught in any transgression, you who are spiritual should restore him in a spirit of gentleness."

The term "restore" comes from the Greek word *katartizete*, meaning "to set him in joint again."[6] When a patient comes to the emergency room with a dislocated limb, often a shoulder, that person is typically in terrible pain. The remedy is provided by a medical professional who can pop the limb back into place. Proper training is required to know where to place pressure. The phrase "firm but gentle" best describes these actions—ram that injured limb toward the socket in anxious frustration and you will induce further damage. The proper procedure is more painful than the dislocation, but only for a moment. Then, as quickly as the pain intensifies, it vanishes. Seeing the relief on a patient's face never gets old.

6   Keller, *Galatians For You*, 167.

When my husband would get angry, I would usually freeze because I feared causing further harm. Then I tried picturing someone with a dislocated shoulder coming to my emergency room for treatment and the physician declining to help him because he didn't want to see his patient's pain increase. That seems ridiculous now, looking at the bigger picture and all that would have been at stake.

I go back to these moments in the exam room when I read Galatians 6:1. We who are spiritual—who have learned of Christ, had the needed instruction, and know enough to help and not cause further harm—can and should restore a relationship in a spirit of gentleness. Not with a shouting match that insists on our own way. Not with persistent meddling because we simply must prove ourselves right to our adult children. I assure you, that will not end well.

Even if your adult child is not a believer, now is not the time for another sermon that he could hand back to you chapter and verse. If he had the opportunity to hear the gospel both at home and church when growing up, you don't need to tell him where he has violated God's word. He knows. What might be a better strategy is what meekness would employ: humbly confessing your frailty both as a parent and as a believer.

Before the hair stands up on your neck, think one more time about Sharon's struggle with shame, with not being good enough. Imagine her hearing her father say something like this:

> You know what? I haven't modeled transparency enough. I sometimes struggle with shame too. I am more sinful than you know. I was given a gift (Christ's righteousness for my sin and shame) in exchange for what I can never do: be good enough. That's why

Christ is so beautiful to me. Forgive me if I've shown you only rules instead of Jesus. Oh, how that breaks my heart if it's true. No one would want to be a part of that. And if I've made you feel small or less than or unloved, I am sorry. I will try to listen to you. I love you regardless of what you believe or do, but it's hard for me when I think your beliefs and actions are going to harm you. I know now that I don't need to nag you about that. But I hope we can talk about it sometime. Until then, I will talk to God, who loves us both more than we can ever imagine. Right now, just as you are, I want you to know I deeply love you. I am an imperfect, flawed parent who does not deserve you, my beautiful child.

There are countless angry adult children who have not spoken with their parents in years. They have a list of grievances, but the one they are afraid to share? Ironically, it's the same pain rejected parents feel—they don't believe they are genuinely loved. Or, if they do feel loved, they don't feel their parents *like* them. There's only one way to address this—to tell your angry adult child that you were wrong and you love them. This may sound crazy, but it's only as counterintuitive as God's kindness that brings repentance (Rom. 2:4). It's only as scandalous as "while we were still sinners, Christ died for us" (Rom. 5:8).

Discussion Questions

1. Can you think of a time when you struggled to control your reaction regarding a choice your adult child made? Did you resolve this? If so, how? If not, how can you cultivate more self-control in this area?

2. When have you hesitated to act because you feared you might make things worse or feared the response of someone involved? What happened?

3. Exhibiting gentleness is not mutually exclusive to giving a rebuke in the right moment or praying with loud cries (as Jesus did). Have you experienced a moment where a rebuke could be considered an act of gentleness?

4. Share a time when God sent someone to confront you about a sin. How did you respond?

5. Sometimes it can be painful to listen to our adult children. We might even fear what they will say to us. When have you dreaded talking to your adult child? What would make it easier?

6. Read Psalm 23 all the way through and then come back to verses 1–3. How does God specifically care for his sheep? According to verse 3, what is our motivation for godly behavior? Have you ever felt your child's exemplary behavior honored you in some way?

9

Faithfulness and Joy

MARCIA WAS TWENTY-NINE and very much alone when she first came to live with us more than a decade ago. Some people have told us we rescued Marcia, but that would be an oversimplification of the story. Though we helped her in a time of need, Marcia has also enriched our family as we walked together through her trials.

Shortly after she moved in with us, her car died in the middle of rush hour traffic on a Friday afternoon. She called me and calmly asked if I could pick her up on the side of the highway. When I arrived, she had one arm stretched over her car hood and one reaching up to heaven. "Lord, you see. Amen." That was it. That was her prayer. She had no more than fifty dollars in her checkbook after she paid her bills. Yet, that was the end of her worry about her car. No hysteria. Not a drop of "What am I gonna do?" in her voice. She hopped in my car, and we called to have hers towed. At a low point that afternoon, Marcia believed God would be faithful to her in her time of need. Me? To be honest, I had my doubts. What does it mean to trust that God will be faithful to us?

Faithfulness

The Greek word for faithfulness is *pistis*. It means "firm persuasion, conviction, belief in the truth, veracity, [or] reality."[1] How does having a firm belief in truth help us trust the Lord? And how does it help us remain committed to others?

In Romans, Paul wrote about the faith Abraham had while he waited on God to keep his promise of making him father of many nations. As the years went by and no baby came, Abraham experienced something counterintuitive: his faith *grew* (Rom. 4:18–22). Faithfulness, for Abraham, meant taking God at his word. God would do what he said in his own time.

But this isn't all that faithfulness means. Faithful people are also trustworthy despite facing difficulty or opposition. While the parable of the sower describes the hearts of those who fall away because of persecution, cares of the world, and the deceitfulness of riches—that is, unfaithful people—the individuals mentioned in Hebrews 11:32–38 show steadfastness in the face of suffering. Hebrews reads,

> And what more shall I say? For time would fail me to tell of Gideon, Barak, Samson, Jephthah, of David and Samuel and the prophets—who through faith conquered kingdoms, enforced justice, obtained promises, stopped the mouths of lions, quenched the power of fire, escaped the edge of the sword, were made strong out of weakness, became mighty in war, put foreign armies to flight. Women received back their dead by resurrection. Some were tortured, refusing to accept release,

---

1   Timothy Keller, *Galatians For You* (Charlotte, NC: Good Book, 2013), 154.

so that they might rise again to a better life. Others suffered mocking and flogging, and even chains and imprisonment. They were stoned, they were sawn in two, they were killed with the sword. They went about in skins of sheep and goats, destitute, afflicted, mistreated— of whom the world was not worthy—wandering about in deserts and mountains, and in dens and caves of the earth.

Abraham is also a good model of this kind of faithfulness. When he and his nephew Lot separated because the land could not support both dwelling together, Abraham offered Lot first dibs on parcels, saying, "Is not the whole land before you?" (Gen. 13:9). Lot picked the choicest area—the lush Jordan Valley just outside Sodom. But this was a mistake, as "the men of Sodom were wicked, great sinners against the LORD" (13:13).

We don't read of any further interaction between these two relatives until Lot was kidnapped by Chedorlaomer and his allies. At this time, Lot and his family had been living inside Sodom. When Abraham heard of the raid, he didn't sit at home and think, "Lot got himself into this mess, he can deal with the consequences." No. Abraham (who was likely near eighty) saddled up 318 men and traveled 175 miles to rescue not only Lot and his family but also "all the possessions" and "the women and the people" (14:16). Abraham's posse brought the entire town back. What took a few verses to mention in the biblical account must have taken enormous effort and courage to accomplish.

Wonder what that conversation between Abraham and Lot must have been like on the ride to Sodom? Abraham didn't appear to hold on to anything but love. He acted at great personal risk, even though his nephew didn't seem to have considered him when choosing the best land. Lot eventually went from living just outside the most evil city in the area to inside it; there's no way Uncle Abraham approved. But, though Lot had not failed to disappoint, Abraham never failed to love.

In writing about this passage, Matthew Henry noted, "Though others have been wanting in their duty toward us, yet we must not therefore deny our duty toward them."[2] If you've ever found yourself in this circumstance as a parent, you may have felt it gut-wrenchingly hard and been driven to your knees. But this situation may have been the Father's plan all along. God is always working both in you and your adult child.

If we have looked at our own mistakes through the lens of God's grace and seen that his perfect will was at work even through our failures, can we not recognize the same with our adult children? Can we not offer them encouragement and a way forward to show we weren't abandoning them just because they made a mistake?

This is sometimes what God calls a faithful parent to do in order to show his love. It may be the very thing your adult child remembers for the rest of her life. It also does not have to be as dramatic as a raid with 318 of your trusted buddies to make a lifelong impression.

When I was home from college, working on a sewing project, I ran out of supplies. My parents weren't home, and the sewing store was just a few miles away. No need to call and ask to borrow the car. I'd be back before I could even contact them.

2   Matthew Henry, *A Commentary on the Whole Bible,* vol. 1 (Iowa Falls: World Bible, 1986), 96.

You know where this is going, right? Before getting out of the store parking lot to drive home, I was startled by a sudden jerk from behind the rear wheel on the passenger's side and the screech of tires. I put the car in park and looked behind me. Great. I'd managed to get in a fender bender. A horn blared, and an angry man jumped out of a Mercedes, walked toward me, and pounded on my window. He had struck my parent's car in the rear and now frantically yelled colorful metaphors at me.

Then I remembered—it was also my parent's anniversary! I made the phone call to my mom that I should have made an hour earlier, but the conversation went a bit differently. "Hello, Mom? Uh . . . happy anniversary! You might need to take the other car to dinner tonight . . . I wrecked the Corolla. I know, I should have asked you about taking the car to the store, but uh, well . . . "

I cringed and waited for the hammer to fall. But my mom didn't ask about the car. "Are you okay? Are you hurt, honey? We can fix a car. The important thing here is you aren't hurt. It is a good anniversary if you are okay. Just please tell me you are alright."

When my dad got home, he looked at the ticket and studied the drawing of the accident. "I don't think this is your fault, Gaye. The officer charged you because you are a twenty-year-old woman and the other driver was an angry, intimidating old man. We'll just see about all that." Later, he took off work to come with me to court.

At sixty-one years old, I still can feel the flood of relief that filled my chest on that balmy afternoon in Charleston. Part of me now knows if I'd placed a call to my parents and waited to hear back from them before leaving, I wouldn't have even been in that accident. But the other part? I would forever know my parents had their imperfect, slightly rebellious, and a tad entitled daughter's back. When any future disagreement tempted me to think they didn't care, I would always remember that accident and their response.

The Opposite of Faithfulness

The opposite of being faithful is being a fair-weather friend. We wouldn't like to think of ourselves as the latter when it comes to our relationships with our children, but we can have blind spots. I listened to a brokenhearted adult daughter tell me that her widowed dad married a woman who gave him an ultimatum: choose me or your daughter and her family. He chose his new bride, hoping that she would eventually warm up to his daughter and her three young children. But she didn't. From the daughter's perspective, she and her girls were traded in for a better offer. They became an inconvenience.

A counterfeit faithfulness can also be appearing to be loving but not being truthful. As mentioned in previous chapters, there is a constant dance between truth and love. Both must be present in faithfulness. We might be busy doing everything in the world for our adult child except the one essential thing: lovingly telling them that they are wrong when necessary. Sometimes a mom might have to use actions instead of words by doing something like not making an expected car payment an adult daughter ought to pay or refusing to cosign a loan a son should never have agreed to in the first place. It may take a mom's behavior (in addition to her words) for her adult child to truly understand what her mom is trying to communicate.

When Abraham saved Lot, he was intervening in order to restrain great evil. But for many parents' situation, unlike Abraham's, rescuing an adult child from a painful situation could interfere with a necessary consequence God uses for that child's instruction. One of the hardest things a parent can do is let their adult child suffer such corrective but redemptive consequences of their own choices. A father may have no idea what his son will do in a particular instance, but what he does know is that his son will grow up, and this may be part of the learning process. The father can walk in humility because he has been there too. He can humbly acknowledge that he has also made mistakes and suffered the consequences. He could even share a story or two to prove it. These can be opportunities for a dad to be vulnerable with his son about his own frailty and sin. If Dad can honestly share some consequences he is currently experiencing, he might also model what it looks like to depend on Christ and to have joy despite his circumstances.

Joy

When the children of Israel grew greatly discouraged at their circumstances—war, outside hostilities, derision, contempt, sin, and constant reminders of their frailty—Nehemiah offered them a bold exhortation: "And do not be grieved, for the joy of the LORD is your strength" (Neh. 8:10). How could they have possibly had joy, given their situation, let alone be strengthened by it? What is meant by joy in the first place?

Joy is "a delight in God for the sheer beauty and worth of who he is."[3] The Greek word for joy is *chara*. It means "joy, rejoicing,

---

3   Timothy Keller, *Galatians For You* (Charlotte, NC: Good Book, 2013), 154.

gladness—bliss."[4] But it does not have to be a natural inclination. Joy is also not the absence of sadness. Even in deep pain, it is possible to experience joy. Read any number of psalms and you will hear the psalmist cry out to God with some of the most gut-wrenching sorrows and questions a heart can know. "My tears have been my food day and night" (Ps. 42:3) and "Has God forgotten to be gracious? Has he in anger shut up his compassion?" (Ps. 77:9) are just two examples among many.

Old Testament scholars call Psalm 88 one of the darkest passages in all Scripture. This psalm doesn't close with a declaration of God's expected victory. No, instead, the psalmist ends with "You have caused my beloved and my friend to shun me; my companions have become darkness" (88:18).

That's real despair. Where is the joy in that? Why put a downer of a psalm like that in the Bible? Its joy is found in this: the psalmist has a God who allows him to be real. He's still praying, still reaching toward his God with honest prayers that show his true emotions—including doubt. God honors that kind of prayer. And it is in the Bible in order to invite us to be this real with God. When we don't see any source of hope, we raise our empty hands heavenward and ask him to fill them.

We cannot stress this aspect of our faith to our adult children enough—that our God is approachable, *that* approachable. He isn't afraid of our doubts and questions. And this may mean God will put us through difficult circumstances where we will have the opportunity to model what this looks like. Years ago, my pastor's wife prayed with me in front of my children, "God, we honestly

---

4   Spiros Zodhiates, Warren Bakker, George Hadjiantoniou, eds., *The Complete Word Study Dictionary New Testament* (Chattanooga, TN: AMG, 1992), 1467–68.

don't know what you are doing, and we don't like it, but we are asking you to help us trust you." She modeled honesty before the Lord for my children and me.

Later, when my kids talked with me about it, far from causing them to doubt, it gave them hope. "God must be pretty cool," Anna said, "to let us come to him like that." I didn't relish the ordeal we were going through, but I loved seeing my kids grow in their faith and find joy in God.

Enjoying God

Many of us were taught the first question and answer of the Westminster Shorter Catechism: "What is the chief end of man? . . . to glorify God, and to enjoy him forever."[5]

In the heart of every soul is a relentless search for joy. It's part of what it means to be made in God's image. Sam Storms wrote, "Enjoyment or delight [in God] is the single most effective means for glorifying and magnifying God."[6] It's not missions work or sacrificial giving or abandoning a lucrative career to go to seminary but utter delight and enjoyment of God. How so?

Joy encompasses our whole being: mind, will, and heart. We are most fulfilled when we focus on God as the sole source of devotion, zeal, delight, gratitude, and hope.

For some of us, this may mean removing our adult child as the chief source of these things. One way a parent can know he has made his adult children the primary source of his joy is in his

---

5 The Westminster Shorter Catechism (1647), Presbytery of the United States, https://www.westminsterconfession.org/.

6 Sam Storms, "Enjoying God," *The Gospel Coalition* (blog), accessed January 20, 2023, https://www.thegospelcoalition.org/.

response to them when faced with losing them to estrangement or death. In that kind of situation, it is understandable to grieve and to do so deeply. However, if Christ is his Rock, he will cling to Christ as he weeps. What if his adult child wrongs him? It's understandable to be hurt. But with Christ, he will not be utterly shaken. Consider Peter's words: "Though you have not seen him, you love him. Though you do not now see him, you believe in him and rejoice with joy that is inexpressible and filled with glory, obtaining the outcome of your faith, the salvation of your souls" (1 Pet. 1:8–9). When Christ is the source of a parent's joy, that parent will be able to persevere with a difficult adult child, a disappointing circumstance, or anything else the world, the flesh, or the devil may throw at them.

I have a dear friend who radiates joy. But she isn't a bubbly, effervescent personality that some might mistake as joy. Because of her calm demeanor, you would never know that every evening she fights a battle on her knees for an adult child who is homeless and addicted to drugs. I've come to understand something about her prayers. As she raises her hands to heaven, night after night and often with tears, the Holy Spirit pours down upon her day after day the strength she needs to keep going, keep speaking the truth in love, and keep praying. Outwardly, she exudes a quiet confidence that comes from joy in Christ. What has this godly mom taught me? When Christ is your center, joy is not optional but inevitable, no matter how trying your circumstance. As 2 Corinthians 4:16–18 says,

> We do not lose heart. Though our outer self is wasting away, our
> inner self is being renewed day by day. For this light momentary

affliction is preparing for us an eternal weight of glory beyond all comparison, as we look not to the things that are seen but the things that are unseen. For the things that are seen are transient, but the things unseen are eternal.

My friend's affliction does not seem light or momentary; her child's addiction has lingered for years. But every evening, she looks again at the unseen—her Savior. Compared to the eternal weight of glory, her burden is light. My friend has discovered the secret: keeping a vision of the unseen future in front of her always.

Joy Supports Faithfulness

Joy and peace are often paired together, with one enhancing the other. But how does faithfulness connect to joy? The writer of Hebrews makes the connection in chapter 12:

> Therefore, since we are surrounded by so great a cloud of witnesses, let us also lay aside every weight, and sin which clings so closely, and let us run *with endurance* the race that is set before us, looking to Jesus, the founder and perfecter of our faith, who *for the joy* that was set before him endured the cross, despising the shame, and is seated at the right hand of the throne of God. (12:1–2)

What enabled Jesus to endure? The joy that was set before him. Now here comes the shocking part—that joy was not only the promise that he would be glorified but also *us*. The God of all creation left perfect bliss to bear unthinkable, indescribable horrors that we all deserved and brought upon ourselves in order to glorify the Father and sit at his right hand—and he did this because we are his joy. He was able to endure because he kept his eye on the prize: us.

I have no clue as to why Jesus would choose us to be his joy, but it wrecks me every time I think about it for more than a minute. I hope I never get over it.

On your worst day, when you feel most unworthy—like you've blown it as a parent, a friend, a spouse, or in any other area of life—get an image in your mind. See the suffering Savior bearing and persevering horrific agonies because he had his eyes on you spending eternity with him. What grace! If we can see our future circumstances as certain, paid for in full by Christ's faithfulness, then we can be spurred on in our own faithfulness with great joy.

Rejoicing in God's Faithfulness

Just a few weeks after Marcia's highway breakdown, a deacon in our church called to tell me about a new car ministry they had started. He was more excited than a mouse in a cheese factory. "It's a bunch of us car guys, Gaye. We procure vehicles from church members who are willing to donate theirs when they are looking to buy a new car. Instead of trading the old one, they give it to us. We look them over, do any needed repairs to make sure they are safe and ready for a new owner, then give them to someone who is in need. We've got a Toyota with a lot of use left in her, ready now. Say, you don't happen to know anyone who could really use a car, do you?"

I looked across the room at Marcia, blinked back tears, and almost stopped breathing. *Lord, you have seen. You have done great things. Great is your faithfulness. We will rejoice.*

Discussion Questions

1. Can you share a time when someone (e.g., your parents, a good friend, the Lord) helped you despite the fact you failed them? How did it make you feel?

2. What is the difference between rescuing an adult child, perhaps to demonstrate grace, and enabling their bad decisions? Can you recall an experience you had like this with your adult child?

3. Read Psalm 71. The psalmist talks to God honestly about his fears (vv. 1, 4, 9–12). Can you describe a time when you had similar fears? What else is this psalm filled with? How does this psalm reconcile both genuine fear and trust in God?

4. Read Psalm 146. Why does the psalmist warn us to not place our trust in man? (vv. 3–4). What kinds of things does God do to bring joy and show how he can be trusted to do what is right (vv. 5–9)? What are some things that interfere with our enjoyment of God? What are things that spur you on to rejoice in the Lord?

5. Nehemiah encouraged a very discouraged people by reminding them that the joy of the Lord was their strength. How can the joy of the Lord be your strength today? What does that look like in your circumstance?

10

Peace and Love

"I MISS MY GRANDCHILDREN. It's been five years since my daughter cut me out of her life with no warning, and I don't know why. She won't talk to me." Tears streamed down a grandfather's face. Family sociologist and professor Karl Pillemer notes that "of all the regrets older people have, a family estrangement is often the most painful."[1]

Though some might tout it as a new phenomenon, family strife is as old as the story of Cain and Abel. However, what we haven't known until recently is just how often estrangement occurs between parents and adult children. In 2022, the *Journal of Marriage and Family* published the results of two studies that followed eight thousand pairs of parents and their children over a forty-year period. Researchers found that one in four adult children in the U. S. had, for a period of time, enacted a no-contact rule with at least one of their parents. Fathers were more

1   Karl Pillemer, *Fault Lines: Fractured Families and How to Mend Them* (New York: Penguin Random House LLC, 2020), 5.

than twice as likely as mothers to suffer estrangement from their adult children.[2]

Angry children. Bewildered, heartbroken, and, yes, angry parents. If there ever was a time when we needed the fruit of the Spirit, it's now. In many homes, the absence of it has only deepened the divide between us. And we have more difficult news to swallow: our giftedness and our personality cannot be mistaken as the fruit of the Spirit.

Spiritual Fruit

It can be easy to depend on natural gifting or personality and call it the fruit of the Spirit, but there are always giveaway signs. Tim Keller, in his commentary on Galatians, explained why this is so concerning in relationships:

> Some folks seem happy and bubbly (joy) and are good at meeting new people, but are very unreliable and cannot keep friends (faithfulness). This is not real joy but being an extrovert by nature. Some people seem very unflappable and unbothered (peaceful), but they are not kind or gentle. That is not real peace, but indifference and perhaps cynicism. It enables you to get through the difficulties of life without being always hurt, but it desensitizes you and makes you much less approachable.[3]

We need to display all the qualities of the fruit of the Spirit, not just our favorite, and we cannot equate our natural gifting

2   Rin Reczek, Lawrence Stacey, and Mieke Beth Thomeer, "Parent–Adult Child Estrangement in the United States by Gender, Race/Ethnicity, and Sexuality," *Journal of Marriage and Family* 85 (December 2022): 1–24.

3   Tim Keller, *Galatians For You* (Charlotte, NC: Good Book, 2013), 153.

or personality with the fruit of the Spirit. It would follow then that we need the Holy Spirit to transform us into the people we ought to be. Let's now look at the last two qualities, peace and love.

Peace

Peace isn't the absence of conflict but the presence of everything we need to flourish. Peace is a "confidence and rest in the wisdom and control of God, rather than your own."[4] Did you catch that last part? "Rather than your own." Any recovering control freaks around here?

We're all familiar with the scene at Martha's house in Luke 10. Martha had welcomed Jesus into her home, where her sister, Mary, sat at Jesus's feet. Martha was left "distracted with much serving" (10:40). In other words, Martha was overdoing it and micromanaging the chaos with her anxious spirit.

And where was Mary? Having her quiet time, of course. It's not every day Jesus joins you live and in person right?

Watching someone with this much focus could make an overloaded control freak like Martha a little nuts. To be sure, Martha was focused too, but with a boatload of cares and concerns she could never maintain alone. She was more than hurt that Mary wasn't helping her. Worse, she chided the Lord with an attitude of "Don't you care?" when she asked him to redirect Mary.

The Lord's response was spot on: "Mary has chosen the good portion, which will not be taken away from her" (10:42). Mary had found the essential thing, out of all the things in that house.

4   Keller, *Galatians For You*, 154.

The Pathway to Peace

How can we let go of control and get the kind of peace that Mary had? Philippians shows us the way as it outlines three steps to gaining peace. The first is to "let your reasonableness be known to everyone," for "the Lord is at hand" (Phil. 4:5). From a Christian standpoint, being reasonable in a given situation may mean thinking of more than what is best just for you. When it comes to our adult children, we can sometimes forget that what is best for us isn't best for them. This means letting go of control. And sometimes, you may have to phone a friend to help you let go.

"I'm not a control freak," my coworker explained. She had been supervising her college senior's packing, right down to rearranging how she folded her underwear. Mom complained about being exhausted, and her daughter was angry over her mom's unwanted instruction. They called me to end their stalemate.

When I surveyed the scene, I couldn't hide my grin. Clothes everywhere, except in a suitcase. What her daughter put in the suitcase, Mom promptly took out; then she went searching for a ziplock bag, a twist tie, or other packing aid.

"Is she like this at work?" her daughter asked me as her mom walked downstairs.

"Um . . ."

"I heard that!" Mom returned; "No, seriously. I'm not a control freak! I just need things done a certain way, that's all." She glared at the suitcase and then looked at me. "And don't raise your eyebrow at me like that!"

I took the ziplock bags from her. "It can be hard to let go, can't it?"

Being reasonable when it comes to your relationship with your child may mean acknowledging that she is grown and can make certain decisions without you—like packing her own suitcase. She may not do it just the way you would. She may forget to pack something important. But that's part of the learning curve for all of us, isn't it? As our kids approach the teen years and onward, we should be looking for ways to let them take the reins instead of offering explanations as to why we need to continue to hover over them.

Step two to gaining peace is to not get anxious (Phil. 4:6). Easier said than done, right? We start thinking about not having anxiety and then we start to have anxiety about having anxiety. Let's look back at the directions Paul gave us: "Do not be anxious about anything, but in everything by prayer and supplication with thanksgiving let your requests be made known to God. And the peace of God, which surpasses all understanding, will guard your hearts and your minds in Christ Jesus" (Phil. 4:6–7). The way to deal with anxiety is to offer it to God in prayer.

Then, step three is God's part. If you follow steps one and two, "the peace of God, which surpasses all understanding, will guard your hearts and your minds" (Phil. 4:7). When we're anxious, it can feel as if the mind is in a perpetual state of chaos. That's the all-consuming nature of anxiety. But God's power is equally all-consuming and up to the task of managing anxiety. It just takes humility for us to let go of our own expectations. This also means letting go of knowing how and when God will take care of what concerns us and acknowledging we are not in control at all.

Having the peace of God during conflict and hardship may mean you don't need to get the last word in on an argument. It may mean you don't ensure your adult son or daughter makes a certain decision you feel is crucial to their lives. Or it may look like making a deliberate decision to daily (even hourly!) focus your mind and heart on God and his word instead of your circumstances. You can change your obsessive focus on your adult child to God; you can entrust your children to the Lord who rules their hearts.

But what exactly does this look like? For starters, it means having a life outside your adult children. How about spending a little longer time in the word and prayer? Is there a church ministry that needs your gifts? If you are married, it might be time to give your spouse some more attention. If you are single, are there friends who could use your encouragement? When my daughter calls, asks me what I am doing on a certain day, and learns I am meeting a friend for dinner, she's thrilled to know my life isn't revolving completely around her and her darling children. And that's a healthier take.

The Opposite of Peace

The opposite of peace is anxiety or worry. Have you ever been stressed while running errands and suddenly forget things you usually have memorized like the PIN to your debit card? Worry is often characterized by the absence of clear thought. Yet, even when we're completely frazzled and could use a break, it's hard to stop believing that God needs help to manage the load. We often make that load heavier by nurturing unrealistic expectations for our family. Expectations are a filter through which parents see their kids from the moment they hold a positive pregnancy test in their hands or get an exciting call from their adoption agency. It's no wonder that parents can grow anxious when their child starts to become a different person than the one they envisioned.

What if my adult son is on drugs? What if my adult daughter married the wrong man? What if my son-in-law is a bad parent? What if my adult daughter and son-in-law tell me they are allowing my granddaughter to change sexes? Our sense of helplessness and hopelessness can overpower us. Don't be anxious. In telling us what not to do, Paul isn't telling us to do nothing. He tells us instead to pray and look to God, especially with God-sized problems like these. Often after a season of prayer, parents have greater clarity on what their next steps should be. They will thoughtfully respond to what life brought them instead of having a knee-jerk reaction. God's word maintains that keeping true peace consists of keeping our focus on God and not our circumstances: "You keep him in perfect peace whose mind is stayed on you, because he trusts in you" (Isa. 26:3).

Keeping the peace may mean resisting our first instincts to "fix" a situation. We fight the urge to grab the phone to call and chew out our child over his choices. We bend our knees and raise our hands to heaven and cry out to God to first do a work in *our* hearts, acknowledging he loves our children far more than we do. Focusing on God may also mean waiting on him to give us clarity of thought as well as unity with our spouse, a counselor, or a pastor before responding to a situation. Or it may mean remembering to be slow to speak and quick to hear when we are in our adult children's presence.

We first trusted in God's wisdom and control when we agreed with him that we were alienated from him and needed to be reconciled (Col. 1:21–22). We trusted God's plan of redemption for us through the finished work of Christ. With our deepest and greatest need met, we should now be confident that we are more deeply loved than we dared dream. And empowered by his love, we can face any earthly tribulation. Our peace with God was purchased through the blood of Christ because of his great love for us, hence peace and love are intrinsically connected.

Love

Paul longed for those he discipled to know the love of God. In Ephesians, he prayed that the saints might comprehend the breadth and length and height and depth of God's love—which, he explained, is beyond knowledge—so they may be filled with all the fullness of God (Eph. 3:14–18). God's love has been poured (not trickled) into our hearts through the Holy Spirit (Rom. 5:5).

Overall, love is the inner disposition out of which the other qualities of the fruit of the Spirit flow. It means to "serve a person for their good and intrinsic value, not for what the person brings you."[5] In my college days, a popular definition for Christian love was "an act of the will." This was supposed to set Christian love apart from infatuation because romantic feelings often wax and wane over the years, but our will, it was thought, could sustain a marriage. Yet this was fraught with its own peril, as our wills proved to be as imperfect as our feelings. What adult child would respond to you giving them a gift on their birthday solely out of obedience to God instead of deep love for them? How devoted does that sound? Love encompasses more than just an act of the will or just an emotion.

Reading 1 Corinthians 13, one of the most celebrated Scriptures on the subject, you get a sense that love is a work of the

5   Tim Keller, *Galatians For You* (Charlotte, NC: Good Book, 2013), 153.

Holy Spirit. How else could one come to be patient and kind and never envy, boast, be arrogant or rude, demand one's own way, or become irritable or resentful (13:4)? How, apart from Christ, could someone consistently bear all things, believe all things, hope all things, and endure all things (13:7)?

If you've ever taken a writing course, you may have heard the adage "Show, don't tell." It's useful here. Before he died, Jesus was brought before the governor's soldiers. Matthew wrote that they gathered the entire battalion (about 120 to 200 soldiers)[6] before him. They twisted a crown of thorns and placed it on his head, stuck a reed in his hand, stripped him, put a scarlet robe on him, kneeled before him, and mocked him. They spit on him, struck him with the reed, and then led him away to be crucified (Matt. 27:27–31). This was cruelty, humiliation, mockery, and betrayal to one who was forsaken and friendless for our sake. This was a picture of love for us. As Romans 5:8 says, "God shows his love for us in that while we were still sinners, Christ died for us."

Our love is not like this. We want to know in advance that our love will be returned. In kind. Even then, we can put conditions on who, how much, and how long we are willing to love. How much of human love depends upon the worthiness or the good behavior of the other person? "If my son would just show some effort at school, then I would be more inclined to love him." Our thoughts aren't that blunt, but our actions might give us away.

Or perhaps when Dad does take the initiative, he pulls back when his son hurls an angry retort at him, questions his true

---

6   Michael J. Wilkins, study notes for the Gospel of Matthew in the *ESV Study Bible* (Wheaton, IL: Crossway, 2016), 2034.

motives, and rejects his love. Dad believes he had every right to pull back. How is that bearing and enduring all things? To clarify, I don't believe God calls us to endure abuse that harms our souls and bodies—whether sexual, physical, verbal, or emotional abuse. But if you never endure difficult interactions with others, how do you reflect something of the love of God?

God loved us while we were still sinners, and he loved us before we loved him. Scripture says, "In this is love, not that we have loved God but that he loved us and sent his Son to be the propitiation for our sins" (1 John 4:10). Jesus took the wrath we deserved on himself.

And he didn't die for perfect people. If we're honest, none of us are perfectly good parents. We grow weary, get angry, lose heart. We take things personally. Our feelings are deeply wounded, and we opt for self-protection rather than what's best for our kids. But Jesus didn't die for perfect parents. He died for parents who needed a Savior and continue to need one. That is real love. Let's look now at its opposite.

The Opposite of Love

The opposite of love is treating someone well to receive something or because they make you feel better about yourself. Parents long to know their adult children love them. These longings aren't wrong until they grow into a relentless, demanding pursuit. When they do, those longings can translate into unrealistic expectations, blind spots, bad decisions, and then disappointment. In a culture that sees children as a commodity that serves the needs of their parents, not image bearers of God entrusted to our care, this can spell trouble.

Loving the Unlovely

While there is no such thing as a perfect parent, there are godly parents who seek their child's ultimate good and yet have ungodly and unloving adult children. Barbara Juliani was eighteen when she left home and abandoned Christianity in search of happiness apart from her family. For years she searched, looking to bad relationships, a live-in boyfriend, expensive houses, clothes, jewelry, and cars, while her anguished parents pleaded and prayed for her. Her dad, C. John Miller, wrote in *Come Back, Barbara*,

> If you struggle with a rebellious child, ask God to show you the power of God in human relationships. From him you will learn the power of God does not consist in the capacity to control others or get your way by playing games. Instead, it begins with the release of love as you forgive your erring child. It expresses itself in the capacity to endure when your love is ignored or even rejected. It is the power to mount a love offensive by doing good right on the heels of being wronged. It is also the power to confront sin with tears and great humility and wait until the day when you see a familiar figure coming down the road toward home.[7]

Barbara did eventually make that walk toward home and brought her husband too. As a result of her reconciliation with her parents, many others came to know the Lord as well.

To love in the way Barbara's parents did requires that you love from a place of fullness. You cannot give what you do not have.

---

7   C. John Miller and Barbara Miller Juliani, *Come Back, Barbara: A Father's Pursuit of a Prodigal Daughter*, 3rd ed. (Phillipsburg, NJ: P&R, 2020), 149.

This is why it's essential to experience and be filled with the love of God.

Jesus Fills Us with Love

Our culture's definition of love encourages us to love someone if they give us joy and drop them when they stop. In contrast, Jesus "emptied himself of all but love" so that he could fill us.[8] He gives to us so that we might be able to fill others with the love we receive from him rather than with our agendas, our anxieties, or our needs in hopes they will in turn fill us. But some of us have been asking our adult children to fill something in our hearts only Christ can fill.

When Jesus was spending his final hours with his disciples, he washed their feet. Washing feet, in that day, was a necessary but unpleasant duty in the home. Jesus, the guest of honor, washed his disciples' feet, including the man who would betray him. He was showing his disciples that true love was laying aside one's life for the good of another, as he was about to do on the cross. But this was more than mere sentiment and an act of the will. Jesus was also invested in the heart: he wanted to see those he saved gloriously restored. He had a vision of who they would be in him. So he did something he did not want to do—suffer and die on a cross—because it was necessary to bring us into fellowship with him.

Hebrews says that "for the joy that was set before him," Jesus "endured the cross, despising the shame, and is seated at the right hand of the throne of God" (Heb. 12:2). This is

---

8   Charles Wesley, "And Can It Be, That I Should Gain?" (1738).

a complete picture of love: emotions, will, and investment. May the Spirit help us resolve to have the same love for our adult children.

Discussion Questions

1. 1 John 4:18 reads, "There is no fear in love, but perfect love casts out fear. For fear has to do with punishment, and whoever fears has not been perfected in love." What kinds of fear interfere with your relationship with God? How does his love cast out fear? How can you reflect God's love to your adult children? What is your greatest fear concerning your adult children?

2. Read Psalm 42. How does David describe his devotion to God in verses 1 and 2?

3. In Psalm 42, David is talking to his heart instead of listening to it. How does David acknowledge both the reality of his sorrow as well as the source of peace (vv. 3–4)? Can you think of a time when you needed to do the same? How did God meet you in that circumstance?

4. Read Psalm 107. There are four descriptions of the ways the people have been scattered (vv. 4–9, 10–16, 17–22, 23–32). Who are the people described in each of these sections? What did God do for them? What does the psalmist suggest a proper response should be?

5. What recurring theme did you notice in Psalm 107? What does this psalm tell us about God's love when we disappoint him? How might that encourage us as parents of adult children?

6. How can a parent relinquish control of his or her adult children, especially if that parent's personality is more like Martha's than Mary's?

7. Why is an act of the will an insufficient definition of love? How might this flawed understanding of love fail you with respect to your adult children?

Conclusion

ONE AFTERNOON AN EXHAUSTED ME went to the grocery store with my colicky baby, Anna, who wouldn't stop crying. I went up and down the aisle without putting a thing in my cart, hoping the lights and sounds at the store would soothe her. An elderly man—who looked to be about a hundred—stopped me and peered into Anna's face. She looked up at him and stopped crying! His eyes watered and tears started streaming across his cheeks. "Them's precious, sweet times when they are that little. But, for me, those years are gone forever."

He had to have been an angel of God because I couldn't breathe for the next two minutes. I picked Anna up and held her tight, whispered I love you, and asked God to help me cherish every single moment I have with her—even when she was screaming. By God's grace, I was going to double up my effort and try even harder to love her right—the way I was supposed to love her, the way she deserved and needed to be loved, always and amen.

Anyone else ever made a vow they couldn't keep? I would quickly learn that my love, however earnest, would be sorely lacking. My husband and I were still sinners, and we brought our sin—however unwanted—into our parenting. If we were going to love our children in a way that would allow them to flourish, we needed to pursue our Savior. Just as we needed to know God better in order to understand ourselves, we needed to return to him again with empty hands to equip us for our task as parents. After all, it was God who had given us our children in the first place.

Our horizontal relationships, adult children included, are best cared for by pursuing our vertical relationship with God. And that is what I have sought to give you in this journey of *Loving Your Adult Children.* I hope by reading this book you've come away with a fresh devotion to your Savior, an understanding of how his love and power equip you to love your adult children.

General Index

Scripture Index

TGC THE GOSPEL COALITION

The Gospel Coalition (TGC) supports the church in making disciples of all nations, by providing gospel-centered resources that are trusted and timely, winsome and wise.

Guided by a Council of more than 40 pastors in the Reformed tradition, TGC seeks to advance gospel-centered ministry for the next generation by producing content (including articles, podcasts, videos, courses, and books) and convening leaders (including conferences, virtual events, training, and regional chapters).

In all of this we want to help Christians around the world better grasp the gospel of Jesus Christ and apply it to all of life in the 21st century. We want to offer biblical truth in an era of great confusion. We want to offer gospel-centered hope for the searching.

Through its women's initiatives, The Gospel Coalition aims to support the growth of women in faithfully studying and sharing the Scriptures; in actively loving and serving the church; and in spreading the gospel of Jesus Christ in all their callings.

Join us by visiting TGC.org so you can be equipped to love God with all your heart, soul, mind, and strength, and to love your neighbor as yourself.

TGC.org